The Meg Fowler Story

by James Youngblood

James Youngblood

DEDICATION

To my wife, Ellie, whose love, devotion and support made this book possible.

Other Books

==========

The Tattooed Hunter

Guarding Patty

An Odyssey of Love

The Throwaways

Astrid

The First Day

The Faux Siblings

The Reluctant Pen Pals

Dario, Charley and Me

The Discovery in the Pines

It Isn't Easy Being Corky White

But for the Choices They Made

Breaking the Cycle

My Spiritual Journey

Unexpected Love

Fates Interlocked

The Jonathon's Destiny Series;
The Quest of Jonathon Roberts, Book 1
Unleashing America's Potential, Book 2

The Duncan Series;
An Unusual Romance, Book 1
The Road to Bougainville, Book 2
Beyond Bougainville, Book 3

James Youngblood

Prelude

When Megan Fowler was thirteen years old, she was brutally raped and badly beaten by her father, Jake. Six weeks after her rape, Meg learned that she was pregnant and Jake had the pregnancy aborted.

Jake was a professional pimp and her mother, Edith, was a drug-addicted prostitute. Jake and Edith both claimed that he was not Meg's biological father; her real father was one of Edith's johns. Their home was frequently used by Edith and Jake's other prostitutes to bring their regular johns to have sex. Jake also sold drugs to his prostitutes out of the house.

This house was the worst possible place to raise a child, especially a pretty young girl like Meg. A year later, August 6th, 1987, Meg's life would never be the same.

1

Meg was having dinner alone, as usual, when Jake came home early, around six-thirty, carrying a Victoria Secret bag. Meg immediately started to worry because Jake seemed unusually happy about something. Meg knew that every time jake was happy or mad, something bad was going to happen. The first thing that came to Meg's mind was rape. It had been a year since Jake raped and beat her; and she worried every day since that he would do it again. Was this the day?

Jake said, "Hey, sweetheart, I've got something nice for you"; and gave her the bag."

Meg heart began beating fast and said, "Please, I don't want it."

Jake said, "Take off all your clothes and put this on. I'll be there in a couple of minutes."

Meg didn't move and Jake got angry. "Goddammit, I said put that on; now!"

Jake started toward Meg and she ran to the bedroom.

"Oh no; he's going to rape me again! I wish I could just die. I'll just let him; I don't want to get beat again. I need to get a knife so I can kill him if he tries to rape me again. I wonder what he wants me to put on? I guess I had better do what he says."

Meg opened the bag and pulled out something small and soft; it was black. She held it up and saw that she could see through it; it was a negligee. *"Oh, crap! Now, I know he wants to rape me! If he does, I'm going to bite and scratch him!"*

Jake bursts into the room and slapped Meg so hard she fell to the floor. He yelled, "Goddammit, I told you to take off your clothes and put that on! Do it right now!"

Crying, and trembling, Meg took off her clothes and started to put on the negligee. Jake hit her and said, "Take off your panties; I want you naked!"

Meg took off her panties and put on the negligee.

Jake said, "Damn you're a hot little thing. I'm going to make a lot of money with you. It's time you contributed to your keep. Men will pay a lot for a pretty young girl like you."

Meg. Instantly knew exactly what that meant; prostitution. She said, "I don't want to be a prostitute like mom!"

Jake said, "I don't give a damn what you want. You are my property and you are going to do what I say. I've got a guy that will pay a lot to have sex with you and he will be here in an hour or so."

Meg shouted, "I won't do it! I'll fight him and scratch his eyes out!"

Jake immediately flew into a rage. He grabbed Meg and tore off the negligee. Next, he held Meg with one hand and took off his pants with the other hand. After his pants were off, Jake hit Meg in the jaw and her stomach and threw her on the bed where he repeatedly raped her.

After Jake finished, he said, "You little bitch, I'll kill you next time. Now, you be good to your customer when he gets here."

Meg was in a lot of pain after Jake left and was determined to not have sex with that man.

"I've got to get out of here before Jake brings that guy home; but where can I go? I'll put on extra clothes and just get out of here as soon as possible."

Meg put on two t-shirts, two blouses and two pair of jeans and her jacket. *"I need some money. Jake keeps some money on the dresser; maybe there still is some money there."*

Meg went to Jake's bedroom and found some bills and change; she put it in her pocket and left. Meg went to a nearby park and hid until after dark. While she hid, it hit her; she had no idea where to go or what she would do next. First, she needed a new name. She chose Mary Smith. She also knew that she needed to say that she was eighteen; an adult. *"That's it; I'm Mary Smith and I am eighteen years old. I'll say that I am from San Francisco."*

As Meg waited for darkness, she began to cry. Next, she was frightened. Frightened or not, Meg was going to get away from Richmond. Things couldn't get any worse for her than staying with Jake and her mom. Meg had never been to church and knew nothing about religion; but she prayed that God would protect her. Somehow, after praying, Meg found courage and began to relax.

11

After it was as dark as it was going to get, Meg walked to the I-80. The first on-ramp she got to was Northbound and she stood there to hitch-hike a ride to anywhere away from here. Finally, a truck stopped and Meg was both glad and scared.

The truck window lowered and the driver said, "Hop in."

Meg's heart was in her throat but she climbed into the cab of the truck. As she got inside, Meg's fingers wrapped tightly around the steak knife that she too from the kitchen. In the dim light, she could see that the driver was a big man and had a big smile. "Where are you headed young lady?"

"Oh, shit! I didn't think about this. What is the name of the next city?"

Meg said, "Vallejo. I'm going to visit my mom in Vallejo."

The driver said, "You must be desperate to be out at night hitch-hiking."

Meg said, "I am; my mom is sick and has no one to take care of her."
The driver said, "Well, you are in luck. I am going through Vallejo but I'll have to drop you off the interstate and get back on it."

Meg said, "That will be okay, thank you."

After a few minutes, the driver said, "You don't talk much, do you?"

Meg looked at him and simply said, "No."

After that, the driver talked non-stop until they got to Vallejo. Meg was watching the road signs when the driver asked, "What exit do you want?"

The next sign read, Tennessee St. so Meg said, "The next one, Tennessee Street."

The driver exited the interstate and pulled into the parking lot of a Seven Eleven store.

The driver said, "I hope your mom will be okay."

"Thanks for the ride, mister."

"You're welcome."

Meg bought a sandwich and a coke. She sat outside the store, ate her sandwich and wondered where to go next. Deciding to keep going farther away from Richmond, Meg got up and started walking back to the interstate on-ramp to hitch another ride.

Meg was on her way to her future.

2

It was one o'clock in the morning, and Pop and Julia had just wrapped up the crime scene. Pop said, "Thanks, Julia, let's get you home; you need to get some sleep."

Julia laughed and said, "I'll give you the same advice. As I recall, you were here right along with me."

Pop said, "No rest for the weary; but I'm ready to call it a night, for sure."

As Pop turned off I-80 at the Tennessee Street exit, he saw a young girl standing in front of a 7-11 store. He pulled into the parking lot. Julia rolled down her window and called, "Hey, young lady; come here."

"No, go away and leave me alone. I'll call the cops."

Julia said, "I am a cop" and showed her badge. Meg nervously asked, "How do I know that badge is real?"

Julia said, "I guess you don't, but we are cops. What are you doing out on the street at this time of the morning? How old are you?"

"I'm eighteen."

"Show me your ID."

"I don't have an ID."

"I thought so. How old are you fourteen-fifteen?"

"I told you; I am eighteen."

"What's your name?"

"Mary Smith."

"I see. Well, Mary Smith, you are going to take a ride to the police station."

"You can't arrest me. I haven't done anything wrong."

Pop said, "Well, miss Mary Smith, I can hold you for seventy-two hours without any charges. Are you coming peacefully; or do I cuff you."

"I'll go."

Pop turned on the dome light to get a better look at the girl; she looked no older than fifteen; if that.

At the station, Pop and Julia led her inside to the desk sergeant and Pop said, "Hold Mary Smith on suspicion of prostitution; we are keeping her 72 hours without charges while I find out who she really is."

While Meg was being booked, Pop went to the bathroom and washed his face. He was dead on his feet but he couldn't go home yet; something about the girl captured his concern for her well-being.

The desk sergeant said, "Miss Smith, I need to search you; hold your hands high over your head."

"Oh shit! He'll find the knife!"

The sergeant said, "Well look what we have here" and pulled out the knife. She is armed. Miss Smith, what do you intend doing with this?"

"Protect myself."

"From what?"

Meg said, "From anyone that tries to do something to me."

The sergeant showed the knife to Pop and Julia and said, "We have a tough one here."

After the girl was fingerprinted, the sergeant took her booking photo and said,

"Her face is bruised and she is wearing multiple clothes".

Pop asked, "Why are you wearing so many clothes?"

Meg defiantly said, "I don't have to answer questions; that's my right."

Julia looked at the bruise then looked into Meg's eyes; they were clear with no signs of drugs. Next, she pushed Meg's sleeve up past her elbow; no needle tracks. Julia checked her over and saw that she was clean, no tattoos; no signs of a typical street girl; just a runaway.

Then, Julia saw something just under her rolled-up sleeve. Julia pushed the sleeve higher and saw what appeared to be a bruise. Julia said, "Come with me" and led the girl to the bathroom.

Julia said, "Is that a bruise?"

Meg reluctantly said, "Yes, ma'am."

Julia thought, *"At least she is no longer seems hostile."*

Julia asked, "Are there more bruises?"
"Yes, ma'am."

The girl pulled off her blouse and Julia saw that she wasn't wearing a bra; but definitely needed one. There were bruises all over her rib cage.

Julia said, "You've been badly battered. Who did this and how long has this been going on?"

After hesitating, Meg said, "As long as I can remember."

"Who did this?"

"My dad; only he and my mom say he is not my real dad."

Julia asked, "You are running away from him, aren't you?"

"Yes, ma'am."

Julia asked, "Did you ever tell anyone?"

"I told the police several times but they never do anything. Each time I told; I was beaten worse. I finally gave up; and here I am.

Julia said, "Okay, put your clothes back on."

After Meg dressed, Julia took her back to the interrogation room and told Pop about the bruises. Now, Pop was more concerned. He said, "Julia, we can't do anything to contribute more to this girl's misery."

Julia said, "I agree. She told me that the beatings have been going on since she can remember."

Pop decided to talk to her again; not interrogate her.

Pop asked, "Now, Mary Smith; you and I both know that Mary Smith is not your name. What is your name?"

Julia said, "Honey, it will go a lot better for you if you are straight with us and answer our questions truthfully."

Meg said, "Mary Smith."

Pop said, "Okay, if that's the way you want it."

Julia asked, "Where are you from?"

"San Franscisco."

"Where in San Francisco?"

"I'm homeless."

Pop and Julia gently questioned her for an hour and were finally convinced that she wasn't going to cooperate. Julia

asked, "Do you want something to eat? How about a burger and fries?"
Pop asked, "With a coke?"

Meg asked, "Yes, and could I please have a root beer instead?"

That's the first time they got a straight answer from her;

Pop said, "Of course, you can. "I'll be back in a few minutes."

Pop bought burgers for her, Julia and himself; neither he or Julia had eaten since lunch yesterday.

Julia took Meg to the bathroom so she could relieve herself and wash her hands.

The three of them opened their burgers and Meg took a bite. She looked at Pop and said, "Thank you. You guys are not regular cops, are you?"

Pop laughed and said, "No, we are Crime Scene Investigators."

Meg said, "That other cop, the one behind the desk, told me that I could trust you; can I?"

Julia looked her in the eyes and said, "You most certainly can. Nothing is going to happen to you; unless you are guilty of something. Are you guilty of anything?"

"No, ma'am. What's your names?"

"They call me Pop."

"Pop? What kind of name is that?"

"A nickname."

Julia said, "I'm Julia. Now, how about you telling us your real name?"

Meg just hung her head and said nothing.

After they finished eating their burgers, Pop said, "Okay, Mary Smith, it's time you go to the lockup."
Meg was immediately frightened and asked, "I have to be in jail?"

Pop said, "Where else would you go? This is a jail; and you have been arrested."

"But I haven't done anything wrong."

Pop said, "You haven't; how about lying to a police officer, filing a false report, carrying a knife and suspicion of prostitution?"

"I would never be a prostitute! That's why I ran away. My dad was going to make me start prostituting."

Julia said, "Honey, you are making this very difficult for you; and it's unnecessary. We are only trying to help you; but you are leaving us no other choice."

Meg said, "You don't know my dad; if I talked to you, he would kill me."

Pop said, "Look, young lady, Julia and I are tired and need some sleep. No one is going to hurt you here; but you are going to lockup."

It was clear that Meg was afraid but there was no other choice. If it were later in the morning, they could call child services; but not at four in the morning.

Pop finally said, "Sergeant, lock her up. Do you have an empty cell you can put her in?"

"Sorry. I only have one cell for women and no empties; she will have to go in there with the hookers."

They walked Meg to the cell block and put her in a cell with three prostitutes.

Julia said, "Pop, I don't like this."

Pop said, "Neither do I but what choice do we have?"

Julia said, "At four in the morning, none." The cell door was locked and Pop, Julia and the jailer walked away.

In the cell, one of the women said, "Look what we got here; fresh meat."

Meg knew these kinds of women and didn't like being in there with them. She also knew that they could be vicious if they were provoked; and she was now very frightened.

There was one woman that appeared to be strung out on drugs and two women dressed very provocative with bleach-blonde hair, and lots of makeup.

One of the women, chewing gum, said, "Look what we have here. Did you rob a bank or something?"

The other woman said, "Leave her alone. Honey, don't pay any attention to her. My name is Flo, what's yours?"

"Mary Smith."

"Okay, Mary, why is a little girl like you in a place like this?"

Mary instantly liked her and said, "My dad is a pimp and he was going to make me prostitute for him; so, I ran away. Two cops found me and arrested me."

Flo said, "Listen to me, honey, you did the right thing. You don't want to end up like us. Never get into prostitution, drugs or alcohol; and get yourself an education, if you can."

Meg said, "I know. My mom is a prostitute and I don't know who my real dad is. My mom says I am not his child. I asked my mom who my real dad was and she said she didn't know who my real dad was; just some john she had sex with."

Flo said, "That's so damned sad. Honey, you can relax in here. I won't let anyone hurt you. You just stay close to me."

Mary felt a little better but the jail, and the inmates, still frightened her. She looked around the cell and the other cells that she could see. She knew that she didn't belong with these kinds of people. *"I swear I will never end up like these people; but what can I do? I'm stuck in here and I didn't do anything. Now, I am going to be put in foster care; and I heard that foster care was as bad as my home. It's more than three years before I turn eighteen and can be on my own. I'll just have to endure; I can do it."*

In the meantime, Pop said, "I don't like having to leave her in there. I know that she is scared; she is just a child and I want to help her. Julia, I can't leave her in there."

Julia said, "We have no other choice."

Pop said, "Yes, we do. I'll take her home; after that, Child Services can take her."

Julia said, "But tomorrow is Saturday. You won't get child services until Monday."

"I hadn't thought about that; but I'll simply keep her for the weekend. Mom can help with her."

Julia said, "Okay, superman, go get her and let's get out of here. I need some sleep."

Pop got the jailer and went to the cell block. The jailer opened the door and said, "Okay, Mary Smith, come with me."

She asked, "Where are we going?"

The jailer said, "This is your lucky day. You are being released into the custody of Detective Petrowski. You should be very thankful; that jail cell is no place for you."

Mary felt a big wave of relief. When they were back at the desk, she said to Pop, "Thank you. Where are we going?"

Pop said, "We are going to my house."

She immediately stopped and said, "Oh, no we ain't; I'm not going to your house. I am not a whore. Go back and get one of the others from that cell and take her home with you. They would be happy to go with you."

Pop laughed and said, "You got it all wrong, kid. My mom is there; and Julia will be too. We don't want you to be locked up with those women."

"Really? That's the only reason?"

Julia said, "Really. No one is going to harm you. Pop is protecting you."

"I hope it's better than a jail cell filled with whores."

31

Pop and Julia brought Meg to his house; and Anna took over. She said, "She's going to be just fine here with me. You guys can go back to work now."

Anna said, "Mary, how about you taking a long hot bath? I'll wash your clothes while you soak. After that, I'll get you something to eat."

"Okay."

"Be sure and wash your hair good and use the conditioner."

"What is conditioner?"

Realizing that she didn't even know what hair rinse was, Anna asked, "Would you like me to wash your hair?"

Mary quickly wondered if this was some scheme to take advantage of her but she, somehow, felt that she could trust Anna and said, "Yes ma'am."

Anna washed and rinsed her hair with conditioner. When she finished, Anna drained the tub, and said, "Now, I believe you need a nice bubble bath to soak in until your clothes are ready; it's scented with Jasmine and roses. I'll be back with clean clothes in a few minutes."

Anna poured some bubble bath in the tub and turned on the water. Meg couldn't believe what was happening when the bubbles began covering the top of the water. Meg said, "This is fun."

Anna smiled and said, "Enjoy yourself, honey. You may do this every day you are here if you want."

"Oh, I do. Thank you so much."

Meg was feeling a lot safer by the time Anna left the bathroom; and all her fear was gone. *"Ah; This feels wonderful. Anna is very nice; and so is Pop and Julia. Living like this would be like living in heaven. Could a foster home ever be like this?"*

33

When Anna picked up Meg's clothes, she saw that they were all tattered. *"I can't believe that this is her only clothes. She needs new ones."*

Anna knocked on the door and asked, "Mary, are you ready to come out?"

"Yes, ma'am."

Meg got out of the tub, wrapped a towel around herself and opened the door.

Anna said, "Here is some deodorant and perfume. Just put a dab of perfume behind your ears; don't overdo it."

"Where do I put the deodorant?"

Anna asked, "You never used deodorant?"

"No, ma'am."

"You just rub some under your armpits."

After Meg was dressed, she felt great; and smelled very nice.

The next morning, Meg took a shower, dressed and went to the kitchen where Pop and Julia saw her in the morning light. She was a very pretty young girl; prettier than either one of them thought.

Meg had breakfast with Pop, Julia and Anna. As she sat looking at them, she felt like a completely different person. She had never had a meal like this; it was like she thought a real family might be like. Meg's mind wandered, *"If only I had a home like this. These folks sure are nice to me; I wonder why?"*

After breakfast, Pop and Julia took Meg shopping for a couple of new outfits and for a pizza.

Meg was in such a good mood that Pop didn't ask any more questions; he wanted the weekend to be as stress-free as possible.

Meg thought, *"These folks sure are nice. Why are they treating me this nice? What do they want? I'm still a little scared of what their intentions might be."*

The weekend had been like a dream for Meg. She had good food every meal, every day; and all she wanted, too. They all were very nice to Meg and she thought, *"This was the best weekend I ever had."*

Monday morning, Pop said, "Okay, Mary Smith, you and I both know that Mary Smith is not your name. Why don't you tell me what your name is so we can get you some help and protect you from your dad?"

Meg simply refused to tell Pop anything about herself. By now, Pop was convinced that the girl was never going to cooperate. He would have to find out who she was the old-fashion way.

Julia asked, "What are we going to do next?"

Pop said, "I guess we will turn her over to Child Services. After that, I'll try to find out who she is and where she came from."

Julia said, "She is a sweet girl. I hope she can get a good foster family."

Pop took Mary Smith back to the jail where he took a regular picture of her.

Do you know this girl?

As Meg stood for her picture to be taken, it hit her that she would be going into a foster home. *"Why couldn't I stay with Pop and Anna instead of a foster home? I know they would be nice to me. I've only heard bad things about foster homes."*

Meg also wondered why she couldn't have been born to nice people like Pop and Julia? Why do some kids get good parents and some are like her? Meg thought it was very unfair. Why are there people like Jake, her mom and the other prostitutes? Why can't everyone be like the Petrowski's
And Julia? Life was a mystery to Meg and she didn't like the world she was born into.

After her picture was taken, Julia took Meg to a conference room.

Meg asked, "Am I really going to foster care?"

Julia said, "I'm afraid so, honey. We have no choice since you won't tell us who you really are."

Meg said, "If I told you who I really am, you will send me back home. I would rather go into foster care; as bad as it could be it wouldn't be as bad as going back home."

Julia's heart was breaking and said, "I am so sorry but Pop and I don't have any other choice."

In the meantime, Pop called child services; then set it up with the hospital to have Mary examined.

Next, Pop called every TV station in San Francisco and Oakland and asked them to show the picture on their evening news shows and ask for the public's help in finding out who she was.

After Pop finished, he went to the conference room and said, "We now have to take you to the hospital to be examined by a doctor."

Meg asked, "Why?"

Pop said, "Because you have been abused and we need to have it confirmed by a doctor; it's the law."

Pop and Julia took Meg to the hospital and Pop told the doctor Meg's story of sexual abuse and physical battery.

At the hospital, the doctor examined Meg and said, "She has definitely been abused. I'll have her x-rayed and we will know a lot more."

An hour later, the doctor said, "There's no doubt about the abuse. She had fractures of both her upper arms; my guess is that it occurred when she was about two years old, plus or minus six months. Next, she has had seven fractured ribs and I think some of them were broken more than once. Lastly, I can't determine if she was ever pregnant but she has definitely had sex; vaginally and rectally. If I had to guess, given what we can see, I would take her word for it. Lastly, the bruises on her body are recent; maybe three or four days ago at the most. It's obvious that this girl has had a very bad life."

Tears were streaming down Julia's face and she said, "We can't let this little girl go back to her family."

Pop called child services and told them what had happened and that she needed protection from her parents.

Two hours later, two people came to the station and asked for Pop.

Detective Petrowski, I am Loretta Murphy of Child Services and this is my partner, Dennis Leary."

Pop said, "Thank you for coming. This is Mary Smith?"

Julia led them to an interrogation room and Pop gave Meg to the jailer and said, "Keep her with you for a few minutes.

After Julia repeated Meg's story, Pop gave Loretta a copy of her medical report.

Loretta only said, "This is a typical story. I hear this shit every day. Now, I'd like to talk to her alone."

Pop brought Meg to the interrogation room and Loretta tried getting information out of her to no avail. Finally, she said, "I guess it's no use. She won't talk to me either; but she can't stay here."

Julia asked, "Is there any way I can have her stay with me?"

Loretta said, "She needs around the clock supervision until her story, and allegations, are verified; do you have anyone at home while you work?"

Julia, dejected, said, "No."

"I'm sorry we can't let you have her."

Pop said, "I have someone at home, may I take her?"

"Is it your wife?"

Pop said, "No, it's my mother. We live together."

Loretta said, "Since you are with the Vallejo PD, I'll officially place her in your temporary custody."

Pop said, "I am trying to find out who she is and where she is from. I'll let you know as soon as we identify her. Hopefully, we will get something from the TV exposure tonight."

Pop signed the papers to keep Meg in his custody and Loretta and Dennis left the station.

The jailer brought Meg out and Pop asked, "Would it be okay with you if you stayed with me for a while longer?"

44

Meg wondered what was going on but she said, "Yes, I would like that."

Pop said, "Good; you will stay with mom and I until we find out who you are. After that, you will be placed in foster care."

Pop didn't realize that telling her that would make her resist even more. Meg thought, *"Now, I will never tell them my real name."*

3

Pop took Meg home and said, "Mom, Mary is going to be staying with us for a while."

"How long?"

Pop said, "I don't know; until we find our who she really is."

Anna said, "Okay, young lady, let's put your things in the bedroom."

Pop went back to work and Anna told Meg, "Honey, hang up your clothes and put your undies in this drawer; then come to the kitchen."

"Yes, ma'am."

After Anna left the room, Meg stretched out her arms and turned round and round to see the room. She thought it was the most beautiful room she ever saw; and it was hers. She looked through the closets then went to the dresser drawers. Next, she opened the top drawer of the chest-of-drawers. The only thing there was a picture album that was, obviously, very old. The cover was coming apart because it was so fragile. Meg wanted to look at it but was afraid to even touch it. She had a hunger to know all about the Petrowski's and Julia. Now, intrigued by the old photo album, Meg knew what she would do; she would ask Anna if she would show it to her.

Meg found Anna and said, "I saw an old picture album in the bedroom; will you show it to me?"

Anna asked, "Why would you want to look at that; it's ancient history."

Meg said, "I want to know all about you, Pop and Julia; you are my new family."

Anna was touched by Meg and her interest in the family. She said, "Of course, I'll show it to you. Bring it to me; and be very careful with it."

Meg brought the album to Anna. Anna said, "Let's go to the kitchen table and look at it there."

Anna gently opened the cover and the first picture was of six people and a little boy.

Meg asked, "Who are they?"

Anna pointed to the man and woman on the left and said, "That's my mom and dad. The two on the right are Peter's mom and dad. Those two young adults are me and my husband, Alek; and the little boy is Peter."

Meg asked, "Pop?"

"Yes, he was three years old. That was 1938.

"Where was it?"

"It was in a town named Lodz in Poland."

Meg asked, "You and Pop were born in Poland?"

Anna said, "Yes. We moved here in 1938 and became American citizens."

Meg said, "Tell me all about you and Pop's family; I want to know everything, please."

Anna said, "Okay; but, before I do, we will look at the pictures."

Anna carefully turned each page and talking about the families and their friends in Poland. After seeing all the pictures, Anna said, "Peter was born Peter Olin Petrowski on July 7th, 1935 in Lodz, Poland. His parents were Arek and Anna Petrowski. The Petrowski's immigrated to the United States on May, 12th, 1938 just prior to the Nazi invasion of Poland and they settled in Elizabeth, New Jersey.

Anna and Peter immigrated to the United States and settled in Patterson, New Jersey where he lived until he joined the US Navy.
Anna and Peter became US citizens in June 12th, 1946 in Patterson, NJ.

Immediately after Peter graduated from high school, he joined the US Navy. After he completed bootcamp in Great Lakes, Michigan, and military police training in San Antonio, Texas, Peter was assigned to duty on board the destroyer, USS Fletcher, DDE-445, on October, 4th, 1954 in Pearl Harbor, Hawaii.

On November 2nd, The Fletcher sailed to the Far East to join the US Navy 7th Fleet operating in the Formosa Straights.

The USS Fletcher was part of an anti-submarine task force supporting the evacuation of Chinese off the Taschen Islands in the south pacific.

Peter served on the Fletcher until July 23rd, 1957, when he was transferred to the Mare Island, Naval Shipyard, in California.

At the time Peter was transferred, he made First Class Petty Officer and was assigned to a crime investigation unit. Peter really liked the work and was very good at it.

Peter had the good fortune to work with two JAG officers (Judge Advocate General) who taught him a lot about forensics and criminal law. Best of all, he had regular interactions with the Vallejo, California Police Department on crime investigations that involved US military personnel.

Peter's four-year hitch (Term) in the navy was coming to an end and he had to decide whether to re-enlist in the navy or not.

Peter decided to talk to a detective he knew in the Vallejo PD about the chances of him becoming a Vallejo police officer. His friend said that he would ask around and see if there were any openings on the Vallejo police force.

Having earned a good reputation with the police department, Peter was immediately offered a job. He left the navy and went to work for the Vallejo PD in June of 1958.

Next, Peter got married. He had been exclusively dating a girl named Bonnie Faye Guidry for about six months before he left the navy. When he told Bonnie that he was getting out of the navy, she asked, "Why?"

"He told her that he liked the work and wouldn't be subject to sea duty every few months."

Peter didn't know that Bonnie liked that he was away for months at a time; he also didn't know that Bonnie was a party girl when he wasn't home.

After police training, Peter was assigned to patrolman duty. On-the-street policing was far different from crime investigation but it gave him valuable experience.

The job injected him into what he called the sub-culture of inhumanity. As a shore patrolman, a typical arrest was a drunk and disorderly serviceman. The first thing Peter learned as a patrolman was that there was no such thing as a routine traffic stop. Further, he soon found out that he would have very few traffic stops. His nightly routine was arresting someone strung out on drugs or for some drunken domestic dispute. Far too often, he and his partner, along with their backup, would have to enter some dilapidated building to arrest someone that was hiding with a gun.

Three months after he left the navy, Peter and Bonnie were married; but there was an immediate conflict between them about his job. Bonnie hated Pop's work hours; he worked either the four to midnight shift or the midnight to 8AM. Bonnie wanted Peter home; not patrolling the streets.

Finally, Peter had enough and told her that he was a cop; it's what he did and it's what he wanted to do. Peter told Bonnie that he was sorry but she knew what his job was when she married him."

They tried to work it out but Bonnie was never able to accept it; and she divorced Peter seventeen months after they were married.

In the meantime, Peter fell in love with Vallejo and knew that he wanted to make his home here; and have me live with him. He had no interest in marriage again and he was even against serious relationships. Peter knew that his work wasn't conducive to relationships and he wasn't going to give up his work.

One day, Peter made his decision and called me, "Hi mom, there is something I want to talk to you about."

I said, "Sure, son, what is it?"

Peter said, Mom, I love my new job, I love Vallejo, and I love being a civilian; so, I've decided to live here permanently."

I said, "I'm glad that you are doing what you love but I'm not thrilled that you are going to stay in California. I was hoping that you and Bonnie might come back here to live."

Peter said, "Mom, I believe you would love it here. I have a solid job and the pay is good; I want you to come live with me. It's time you retired, anyway."

I said, "Peter, I'm not old enough to retire; besides, I can't live with you and Bonnie."

Peter said, "Oh, I forgot to tell you; Bonnie has filed for a divorce and I'm not going to contest it; our marriage was a mistake."

I said, "I'm sorry. Why don't you come back home? I'm sure you can find a job here."

He said, "Mom, I told you, I like it here a lot better than New Jersey. Mom, I know this is a big decision but you and I are all we have; just the two of us. We should be close to each other; plus, you can retire if you want to or you can work; it's up to you. I just want you here with me; please think about it."

What Pop didn't know was that I actually welcomed the idea. I was still in great shape and was tired of living alone; and I wasn't interested in getting married again. Right now, all I did was work to live and live to work. I was sad about Peter's marriage but I relished the idea of living with him and taking care of him.

A week later, I called and asked, "Is your invitation to live with you still open?"

"Absolutely! You are coming?"

"I told him that I decided that I would like that. I said I was ready."

Peter said, "Wonderful! I'll take some vacation time and come get you."

I said, "Son, you don't need to do that. I am only going to bring my clothes and a few things that I can have shipped. I will fly there by myself."

I moved from New Jersey on November 12th, 1960.

On the flight to San Francisco, I thought, *"Am I doing the right thing? A forty-five-year-old woman living with her grown son? If I like Vallejo, I'll get a job; if not, I'll go back to Jersey."*

After I got there, it didn't take me long to settle in; and Peter told me that he loved having me with him.

I really liked the better weather in Vallejo. Jersey already had a light snow and freezing weather; the day I got to Vallejo, the day was sunny and the temperature reached 76 degrees by noon.

After a month, I was becoming stir-crazy so I found a job in a Dentist's office. I soon made a couple of friends and I liked my job.

By March 3rd, 1961, Peter had been a patrolman with the Vallejo PD for three years when the police chief called him in and asked, "Peter, how would you like a different job?"

"A different job? What job?"

The chief said, "You have done a good job as a patrolman but I believe we are wasting your talents. I would like to offer you a promotion to detective; working vice. Does that sound interesting to you?"

Peter eagerly said, "Yes, sir. Thank you, sir."

That began a whole new career for Peter. Something else that was new was that, because of his initials being POP (Peter Olin Petrowski), everyone had begun calling him Pop again; the same as they did in the navy. The truth is, Peter loved the nickname.

Peter quickly distinguished himself in his new job because of his understanding of crime scene evidence and he always took steps to identify and protect evidence. His effort resulted in several convictions that otherwise wouldn't have been possible; that included two cold cases. He had already been fascinated with forensic science and he knew how important it was to protect the crime scene so evidence can be gathered.

Peter began reading everything he could find on forensics. Because of this self-study of forensics, in January, 1962, Peter was sent to school for forensic training in New York City.

After his training, Peter became the Vallejo PD CSI (Crime Scene Investigator) in the newly formed department. Now, Peter was really happy with his life.

Peter was a handsome man by any measure, fun to be with and a solid citizen. Peter still had his share of time with the ladies but never brought a girl home to meet me.

Peter and I both remained single and happy, just the two of us, until he got a new partner named Julia Archer. That brings us to the present; and the end of the story."

Meg loved the story and felt a lot closer to Anna. Meg went to Anna, put her arms around Anna and said, "Thank you so much for telling me about you guys."

Anna couldn't help but notice the tears falling down Meg's cheeks and held Meg tight for a long time.

Meg was feeling a lot of strange new emotions. Her heart was bursting with love for Anna. This was the first time Meg ever had any kind of intimacy and could feel the love coming from Anna. Meg prayed, *"Please, God, let me stay here forever. Don't let anyone take me away! I'll be good; I promise."*

Anna broke the mood by saying, "Honey, let's get some lunch."

Meg wiped her tears on each shoulder and said, "Okay."

4

As the days passed, there had been no filings for missing girls in the days up to finding Meg or since. All Pop was sure of was, that Mary Smith was not her name and she didn't come from San Francisco.

Julia said, "Assuming everything else she told us is true, I think she is a pretty street-smart girl. If she is as smart as I believe she is, we can eliminate any place north of here; because it's a long way north before there is any significant crime area.

She was on the northbound exit side of I-80. That would indicate that she came from south of here. Since she could get on I-80 in San Fransisco it could be true. However, she could have come from Richmond or Oakland as well. Given her story, and if she is street smart and came from Oakland, she wouldn't go north because Richmond is very crime-ridden; she would go east. Since she ended up here, I believe she most likely came from San Francisco or Richmond; this seems logical to me."

Pop said, "Makes a lot of sense. I'll send her picture to San Francisco, Oakland and Richmond PDs and see if they can identify her. Maybe someone will recognize her."

Meg's picture was shown on all TV stations all afternoon and evening and it generated more than a thousand leads that all went nowhere. After all the leads were run down, Pop and Julia were back where they started.

Pop said, "I can't believe nobody knows her."

Julia said, "I can believe it. She has most likely been a prisoner in her own home. That's especially true if the girl has tendencies to be defiant."

Pop said, "Well, I, for one, believe she can be very defiant."

Julia said, "Maybe you should just turn her over to child services? You've done all you can."

At the end of their shift, Pop said, "I'm getting out of here. I am tired and hungry. I know you want to see Mary so why don't you come for dinner?"

"I would like that, thank you."

Pop pulled into his driveway and Julia pulled in behind him. They got inside the house and found Meg in the kitchen helping Anna. Pop kissed Anna and asked, "And, how is Mary Smith?"

Mary excitedly said, "Hi Pop. Hi Julia. I'm having a lot of fun. Anna took me shopping and she is letting me help with dinner; and she told me all about you."

Pop said, "She did? I'm in a lot of trouble now."

Meg quickly said, "She didn't say anything bad."

Pop said, "Good. I'm also glad that you are feeling better. Are you ready to talk yet?"

Meg's happy demeanor immediately soured and she became silent. Pop regretted killing her festive mood and said, "I'm sorry. You don't have to tell me; I won't ask again."

Meg felt better but her mood remained down and Meg gave all her attention to Anna and Julia for the rest of the evening. It was obvious that Meg really liked Anna and seemed to like Julia. It was equally obvious that she was leery of Pop; no matter what Anna had told her about him.

Pop decided that the best course of action would be to just let nature take its course; and act like a loving parent.

The next day, Loretta, from Child Services, said, "Since we can't find out who she is, we can't establish that the girl actually lives in San Francisco. Therefore, since she was picked up here, she will remain under your care until we know who she is."

Pop asked, "Does that mean we can keep her indefinitely?"

Loretta said, "No, that's for a judge to decide. I scheduled a hearing for five weeks from Monday. The judge will decide what to do with her at that time. In the meantime, she can remain in your custody if you still want to keep her."

Pop said, "Good; we'll keep her."

That night, Pop said, "Mary, there is going to be a hearing in five weeks where a judge will decide what will be done with you. Until then, you will be staying here with mom and I. Is that okay with you?"

Meg quickly said, "Yes, I would like that." Pop said, "I have to say that, if you still persist in saying your name is Mary Smith, it won't go so well with the judge."

Meg remained silent and Pop decided not to press her.

Julia came to Pop's every day after work and on the weekends. During these weeks, it seemed to Meg that they acted as though they were all one family. Meg was happy for the first time in her life. She started loving all three of them; and the three of them, fell in love with Meg.

Pop, Anna and Julia agreed to learn as much about Meg's likes and dislikes as possible without asking who she was or where she came from; they just wanted to know her as a person; and the more they learned about her, the more they came to like everything about her.

They all agreed that Meg was a good-hearted, and loving, young girl; and she had not yet been psychologically or emotionally, ruined.

It was amazing to Meg that she never once thought about Jake or Edith. All Meg cared about was staying with the Petrowski's.

Meg and Julia became closer to Julia than Anna. To Meg, Anna felt like her grandmother and Julia felt more like what Meg thought a mom would be like. Most amazing of all was that Meg began to like Pop. Meg soon began fantasizing that they were her family. All three of them, Pop, Julia and Anna hugged Meg every morning and every night before she went to bed. Meg loved spending each day with Anna but she looked forward to Pop and Julia coming home from work.

James Youngblood

The Monday before the hearing, Julia said, "Mary, you and I are going to buy you a new outfit for the hearing. You need to look your best."

Meg said, "Okay"; but she realized that the judge might take her from them. Meg was getting depressed by the day. She wondered what would happen to her if the judge sent her to a foster home; or worse, sent her back to Jake and Edith.

Two days before the hearing, Pop and Anna met with the judge and told her Meg's story and that she had been a model citizen since she has been with them.

Judge Stacy Langley said, "Thank you for your inputs. I'll render my decision it at the hearing but, first, I want to talk to Mary."

Anna said, "Your honor, if you can find it in your heart, please let her stay with us. We have come to care very much for her and we don't want her to be sent back to be abused again."

Judge Langley said, "I understand how you feel but I must follow the law. Now, "I would like to meet with Mary in my chambers; just the two of us. It won't take long."

In her chambers, the judge asked, "Mary, are you still insisting on keeping your real name a secret?"

"Yes, ma'am."

"Why?"

"Judge, my dad is not my real father and he beats me for no reason except that I won't be his prostitute. When Jake gets mad at anyone or anything, he takes it out on me. If I go back to him, he will most certainly beat me; and maybe even kill me. I only feel safe with the Petrowski's because they love me and don't want me to be hurt again."

The judge asked, "Are you telling me that you want to live with the Petrowski's?"

"Yes, ma'am. I would like to live with them forever; or at least until I am an adult and can live on my own."

It was the day of the hearing and Meg, Pop, Anna and Julia were very anxious; and afraid of what the judge would decide.

The judge opened the hearing and said, "After reviewing the evidence in this case, I find that Mary Smith has been consistently abused but the perpetrator of the abuse can't be determined based on evidence. Since the evidence does show that she has been often abused over a long period of time, it is the decree of this court that Mary Smith remain in the home of Peter and Anna Petrowski as her foster parents until her identity can be established."

Mary turned and hugged Pop, Anna and Julia. She said, "I love you guys."

Three weeks later, Pop received a phone call, "This is Fred Garner from KCRT Television. I just received an anonymous call from a trucker who said that he picked up that girl on the I-80 just inside Richmond heading north. He said she told him that she would be visiting her sick mother in Vallejo. He said that he dropped her at the Tennessee Street exit just inside Vallejo; then hung up. I hope this has merit."

Pop said, "It's does; it validates some of her story. Thank you very much."

Pop found Julia and said, "We hit paydirt! She is from Richmond."

"What's her real name?"

"All I got was that a trucker picked her up in Richmond. She has to be from there."

Julia said, "I don't see how that proves she lived there."

Pop said, "It eliminates everywhere else. We can now concentrate our effort to Richmond."

Pop called the Richmond PD and told them that the girl was definitely from Richmond so someone there has to know her. If her dad is a pimp, how many pimps do you have working the streets in Richmond?"

The vice detective said, "I'd say there are around twenty professional pimps but there are numerous freelancers. I'll have my guys contact all the ones they know."

The next day, the detective called Pop and said, "Nobody is talking. The way they are not talking leads me to believe that she is from here and I am sure some of those guys know who she is; they just won't talk to cops. Sorry."

Pop got a look on his face that made Julia think he had an idea. Julia asked, "What's next?"
Pop said, "You and I are going to school."

"What do you mean, going to school?"

Pop said, "We are going to talk to every eighth-grade teacher in Richmond, if we have to. If she is from Richmond, that's how we are going to find out who she is."

"Great idea."

Pop and Julia went from school-to-school interviewing second grade teachers. They had interviewed nine teachers so far and no luck.

At the tenth school, the teacher looked at the photo and claimed she didn't know the girl; but Julia read her body language and was sure that she was lying. After their interview, and they were back in the car, Julia said, "I know that teacher is lying. I'm sure that is Mary's teacher; but why would she lie about it?"

Pop said, "My guess is that she has been threatened. You can bet that her father saw her picture on the news. The question I have is why doesn't he want her to be identified?"

Julia asked, "Maybe he is afraid that if she is identified, he will be charged with rape."

Pop said, "You're probably right."

Julia said, "That must be the reason."

Pop said, "Let's go talk to the principal."

Pop and Julia got to the principal's office and the principal's secretary said, "I'm sorry, you will have to make an appointment."

Pop, showed his police badge, said, "I don't think so. This is a matter of urgent police business, and we need to speak to the principal; now!"

The secretary excused herself and went inside an office. A few seconds later, she and the principal came out and the principal asked, "Officers, what is the problem?"

"May we speak privately?"

"Yes, please come into my office."

They sat down and the principal closed the door.

Pop said, "We are looking for the identity of this runaway girl and we believe she was one of your eighth-grade students; Mrs. Wells' student."

Pop showed the picture to the principal.

The principal, Mrs. DeGraff, said, "She looks familiar but so do a lot of girls. I'll ask Mrs. Wells."

Julia said, "We already asked Mrs. Wells. She denies knowing her but I believe she is lying."

Mrs. DeGraff asked, "Why would she lie about this?"

Julia said, "We don't know unless she has been threatened."

Mrs. DeGraff said, "I'll get her in here and get the truth."

Mrs. Wells came into the room and, when she saw Pop and Julia, she was clearly upset.

Seeing Mrs. Wells' reaction, "Mrs. DeGraff said, "You know this child, don't you? Tell us the truth; I don't want to ask the children."

"Mrs. Wells lowered her face and said, "Yes, ma-am. She was in my class but hasn't been in school for some time; she dropped out without a word."

"Why did you lie to these officers? That can get you into a lot of trouble."

After a moment of hesitation, Mrs. Wells said, "Her father came to my home and threatened me and my family if I ever told anyone that his daughter attended this school."

Mrs. DeGraff said, "You should have come to me. We could arrange for protection and had him prosecuted."

"I am so sorry. I am afraid of that man."

Pop, getting a little irritated, said, "What's her real name?"

Mrs. Wells said, "Megan Fowler, she goes by Meg. Her dad's name is Jake and her mother's name is Edith."

Julia gave Mrs. Wells a business card and said, "He won't know how we got her name but if he ever comes around again, call me."

Pop said, "Better yet, will you press charges against him?"

"I'm afraid to do that; he is a very bad man."

Pop said, "Okay, don't worry. We already have enough to charge him; and we will send him to jail for a long time."

On the way back to the station, Julia said, "Meg Fowler; I like that a lot better than Mary Smith."

"So, do I. Maybe, now that we know her real name, she will open up. I want to know the whole truth about everything in her life."

Back at the office, Pop ordered a police record check on Jake and Edith Fowler.

In the meantime, Pop and Julia went home to tell Meg the news. After they got there, Pop said, "Hi, you two; how was your day?"

Meg said, "Okay."

Anna said, "We did a little shopping for Mary."

Pop said, "You guys come to the living room. I need to talk to you both."

Both were puzzled but followed Pop and Julia to the living room and sat down.

Pop said, "Julia and I have had a very productive day. We got a call from a guy in Richmond that said he knows Mary. Could he know you, Mary?"

Meg's heart went to her throat and it felt like it was going to burst. She immediately lowered her head and wouldn't look at any of them; and remained silent.

Julia asked, "Is there anything you want to tell us?"

She looked at Pop and whispered, "I'm so sorry; please don't send me back there. Mary Smith is not my real name."

Pop put on his question mark face and said, "Really? It's not Mary Smith?"

Meg said, "My name is Meg Fowler; and I'm from Richmond, not San Francisco. I am fourteen and I ran away from my dad, Jake. He wants me to start prostituting for him; that's why I ran away. He is a pimp and my mom is a drug addict and one of his prostitutes. She is usually on the streets but when she comes home, she sleeps in her own room. Dad has another whore, her name is Juanita Moreno, sleeping with him. Please, don't send me back there. I don't want to be a whore like my mom or a drug addict; I would rather be in jail. It's bad enough to have to have sex with my dad but I don't want to be his prostitute like my mom."

Pop and Julia were blown away and Julia turned to Meg and asked, "You have sex with your dad?"

"Yes. He makes me do it. He started making me do it when I was thirteen; he raped me. I got pregnant and he got me an abortion. Now, he told me that I am old enough to start earning my keep; and that I had at least five to ten good years to make him big bucks. He said that he gets more money for young girls."

Pop asked, "Do you take drugs?"

Meg emphatically said "No. Dad wants me to use drugs but I refuse to take them. I don't want to end up like my mom; he makes her do that. Now, mom is a heroin addict and works the streets. Please don't make me go back there."

Pop's heart went out to her; and he was getting angrier by the minute. He said, "Don't worry, Meg, I won't send you back. Please know that you are safe here."

Julia watched Meg and saw that she looked like a very wholesome young girl that didn't even know how to spell sex. She wondered how people could do such a thing to a girl so young, especially her own parent.

What impressed Julia most was that Meg seemed to be a very sweet girl despite everything that has happened to her.

That afternoon, Meg told Pop, Anna and Julia her life story.

She said she had been surrounded by booze, drugs, prostitution and crime all her life. She was also often left alone, as far back as she could remember.

Meg said, "I was always told to be seen and not heard; If I cried or made any sound, he would beat me. I learned to stay out of sight and never make a sound; but sometimes that didn't help. If he was drunk, or high, or mad about something else, he would take it out on me. Mom said that he even broke both my arms when I was a toddler; just because I wouldn't stop crying.

Mom was good to me until I started school. After that, she got more messed up with drugs and started having men come to the house. I came home from school many times to find mom in bed with some guy. Once, I came home and she was in bed with three men. She asked me if I wanted to join them and I ran outside and stayed until after they left. Mom just laughed at me.

A couple of years ago, mom began walking the streets looking for johns; she was getting too old and that was the only place she could get johns.

Sometimes, she wouldn't come home for days and dad would often bring his hookers home with him. If mom came home when there was a hooker in bed with him, she would just sleep on the couch.

One time, she got in bed with them while they were having sex; it was disgusting!

When I was six, dad made mom stay home and go through detox and I had to stay home and take care of her and I was kept out of school for the entire sixth grade.

When Meg stopped talking, Anna asked, "Honey, what grade are you in now?"

"I just finished the eighth grade."

Anna said, "That's unbelievable."

Meg quickly said, "I'm not lying; it's all true."

Anna said, "Child, Julia is not questioning you; she just means that she doesn't like to believe people could do such a thing. Peter, she must never go back to that world."

They talked until almost ten o'clock and Pop said, "I don't know about you ladies but I need my beauty sleep. I'll see you all in the morning; goodnight."

Julia said, "Me too."

Meg said, "Thank you all for everything; I'm sorry, goodnight."

Anna said, "I'll come tuck you in."

When Meg was in bed, Anna kissed her on her forehead and said, "Sleep well, honey."

"Good night, Mrs. Petrowski."

"Meg, you may still call me Anna."

The next day, Pop asked, "Meg, exactly what caused you to run away that day?"

Meg said, "This is what happened; dad came home for lunch and he was in a great mood. After lunch, he said, "Meg, let's go to bed.""

I knew what that meant; sex.

I said no and he beat and raped me. When he finished, he acted like nothing happened and said, "I have good news. Today, I've got a guy that will pay a lot of money to have sex with you. I told him that you are still a virgin so, when he puts it in you, cry a little and tell him that it hurts. It's time you started contributing money. I can get premium money for you until you turn eighteen, so, you will now be one of my working girls."

I yelled, "I don't want to do that! I hate that."

Dad said, "Don't worry honey, I'll give you something to make it all okay."

"I don't want your damned drugs either. I don't want to end up like mom and your other whores."

Dad said, "Now, don't you worry. Everything is going to be just fine; you'll soon get used to it."

I said, "But I don't want to."

Angry now, dad said, "I told you that it's time you start bringing in money; you don't have a choice. It's your job so get over it. Take a shower and put on something nice. I'll be back in an hour; and you had better be nice to him or you will get what I give your mother."

I knew what that meant; another bad beating. I also knew that this was when I had to leave. I put on two pair of panties, three blouses and two pair of jeans. I took thirty-four dollars and twenty-seven cents from the dresser, two sandwiches and left for where, I didn't know; I just knew I had to leave.

I went to the north on-ramp of I-80 and put out my thumb; ever watching for the cops. I stayed there until a trucker stopped and picked me up. Then you found me.

Julia said, "Meg, honey, we understand why you lied; and it's okay."
Pop said, "Meg, your medical examination confirms your story so everything is going to be fine. You did exactly the right thing by leaving even though I don't like how you did it; you should have gone to the police."

Meg looked at Pop and said, "I told you that I went to the police twice and they did nothing but send me home with jake and more beatings."

Pop, realizing that he was wrong said, "You're right, Meg, I was wrong; you had no good choices and I am proud of you."

Meg thought, *"Finally, Pop believes me. I know it's hard for people to believe."*

A big relief came over Meg and she felt different; she felt like the world had been lifted off her shoulders.

5

In the meantime, back at home, Jake brought the john to have sex with Meg and she wasn't there. Jake sent the guy away and started yelling. "Meg, where the hell are you?"

Jake went outside as if he could somehow see where she went. He thought, *That little bitch ran away! Where would she go? She doesn't know anyone except her mom.*

Jake knew where Edith was on the street and went there. He asked, "Edith, have you seen Meg? Was she here?"

Edith said, "I ain't seen her, why are you asking me?"

"That little bitch ran away. Where would she go?"

"Well, she ain't in here; that's all I know. Give me some money."

Frustrated, Jake went back home hoping that Meg came to her senses and came home; she didn't.

A week later, there was a knock on Jake's door. He opened the door and a man and woman were there. The woman asked, "Are you Jake Fowler?"

"Yes."

My name is Loretta Murphy and this is Dennis Leary of Richmond Child Services. Do you have a daughter named Meg?"

"Yes, why?"

"Don't you know that she is missing?"

"No, I thought she was with her mother."

Dennis said, "Well, she isn't. She is in a Vallejo foster home. She says she ran away from you because you beat and raped her; and you wanted her to be a prostitute for you."

Jake laughed and said, "That girl has a wild imagination. She is always dreaming up some kind of crazy story. I assure you that something like that would never happen. That girl lives in her own fantasy world. Thank you for letting me know. If you will tell me where she is, I'll go bring her home."

Loretta said, "I'm sorry, Mister Fowler but we are required to investigate her claims to be sure her allegations aren't true; you understand, don't you?"

"Of course."

Loretta asked, "Is your wife home?"

"Sorry, she is out."

Dennis asked, "May we come inside and look around?"

Jake said, "Sure, no problem. Sorry for the mess; my wife hasn't cleaned yet."

They looked through the house and Loretta said, "Thank you, mister Fowler. We will be in touch."

After they left, Jake knew that he had better clean things up; and he needed Edith to get clean and stay that way until Meg was home again. He knew that he hadn't seen the last of Child Services.

Jake found Edith and, as nicely as he could, said, "Edith, honey, I need you to come home. I found out where Meg is and we will lose her if you don't come home. You need to be living at home; at least for a while. I'll be good to you, I promise."

After more cajoling, Edith finally agreed to come home. She said, "Jake, you better treat me good or I'll tell them folks what you do to that kid."

"Edith, I'll treat you, and Meg, very nice from now on. I want us to be a family again. Would you do that for me?"

Edith asked, "Will you help me stay sober? I want to sober up and get off the street."

"Yes, I'll help you."

All the time, Jake thought, *"Yeah, I'll help you; till the minute I get Meg back."*

When Edith and Jake got home, Edith immediately started cleaning the house. It felt good to be off the street and getting sober; and she wanted to get sober so bad she would put up with Jake's abuse.

A couple of days later, Loretta and Dennis paid a surprise visit to the Fowlers. Edith opened the door and asked, May I help you?"

"Are you Mrs. Fowler?"

"Yes."

Loretta introduced herself and Dennis and asked, "Is your husband home?"

Edith said, "No, he is at work."

Dennis asked, "Where does he work?"

"He works for himself. He is a consultant."

Loretta almost laughed out loud but controlled herself. She said, "I see. Mister Fowler told us to come back when you were home. We would like to talk to you about Meg."

Edith said, "Please come in."

Loretta and Dennis were surprised to see the house so clean. Dennis asked, "May I look around while you two talk?"

Edith said, "Sure, help yourself."

The entire house was spotless and there was plenty of food in the pantry and refrigerator and Dennis began to have doubts Meg's story.

Loretta said, "Mrs. Fowler, I'm sorry for being blunt but we had reports that you were living on the streets."

Edith quickly said, "I did when I was into drugs. But I am sober now and living with my husband again."

Edith leaned over close to Loretta and said, "I'm sorry to say that, when I was drugged out, I did some things I'm not proud of."

Loretta said, "Well, I am happy that you have your life back."

Edith asked, "Ma'am, when can we get Meg back home?"

Loretta said, "That will depend on the judge. You have a hearing set for October 12th."

"Why so long?"

"The courts are very busy. I'm sorry."

Edith asked, "Can I go see her?"

Loretta said, "No, I'm sorry. Right now, she doesn't want to see you or come home.
I believe this can be a good cooling off period. The judge will decide what the next step will be."

Edith said, "We want her back home as soon as possible. Do you think the judge will let her come home? You know school will be starting soon."

Loretta said, "All I can say is that what we see here looks good. However, I will advise you that we will be coming back to check on you."

"When?"

"Mrs. Fowler, our visits are never planned. We don't want you to clean things up just for us; so, you never know when we will come or at what time. We have to believe that your husband and you are now living in a good relationship. Right now, Meg tells a pretty bad story of life here. We can't take any chances."

When Jake came home, Edith told him about the visitors and the court hearing.

Jake said, "Damn. I don't like this; they might not let us have her back."

Edith looked at Jake with a surprised look and asked, "Why do you even care? I don't."

Jake said, "Because she will bring a good price for the next couple of years. I'll get her back one way or the other."

6

Currently, in Vallejo, Pop and Julia take Meg everywhere and treat her like she is an innocent young girl. Meg loved it because she had never been treated like a little girl; this was all new to Meg. Nice as it was, Meg wondered why they were treating her so good. All she could think about was that she would soon be sent back to Jake. Next, Meg began thinking about running away again. This time, she intended to be prepared. She knew where Jake hid some of his money so planned to steal a lot of money next time. Then, she needed to pick a place to go that was a long way from Richmond; maybe Las Vegas or even Florida.

Pop, Julia and Anna began to really care for Meg and didn't want her to go back her parents.

One day, Julia asked, "Pop, what if the judge sends her back to them?"

Pop said, "If they send her back, there's nothing we can do."

Julia said, "That's a damned tragedy."

Pop said, "Julia, face it; it's out of our hands."

The next day, Loretta called and said, "The Fowlers have petitioned the court to have Meg returned to them before school starts."

Anna asked, "How can they do that after all he did to her?"

"Mrs. Petrowski, parents have rights until they prove that Jake did what Meg alleges."

Anna said, "Don't the x-rays and the medical reports prove that?"

"No; all they prove is that Meg has been abused, not who did it."

Anna, exasperated, said, "Meg told us who did it."

Loretta said, "It's common that kids make up these kinds of stories when they are angry about being punished. The court needs evidence that proves he, or her mother, did those things. Jake claims that, if Meg was abused, it was by Edith. Further, he says that the reason Meg isn't pointing to her mother is because she is afraid of Edith. He said that Meg blames me because she knows I won't hurt her; that's a strong argument in his favor. It boils down to a he said-she said. Having said that, the judge is reluctant to sending her back and we pleaded for time. I argued that there wasn't any proof that Jake didn't do it; but that argument can't hold up in court. You can't prove a negative."

Anna asked, "How can she be protected if she is sent back to them?"

Loretta said, "The judge will return her to them subject to being monitored by child services. It's like a probation; only it's the parents that are on probation. If child services see anything suspicious, Meg would be returned to foster care."

Anna asked, "Does that mean back to Peter and I?"

Loretta said, "No, ma'am; she would be placed in foster care in Richmond."

Pop said, "Mom, it is what it is. I'm sorry."

Anna said, "Well, I think this is a load of crap. What happened to Meg's rights?"

Loretta said, "I'm sorry, Mrs. Petrowski."

They all were upset that Child Services was defending her father's rights. One day, Pop asked, "Julia, why the hell do they want to send her back to that bastard?"

Julia said, "Because they, obviously, don't believe Meg. The reports we get from Richmond insist that the home is clean and both parents live together; and they have never found them drinking or high on anything."

Pop said, "If Meg is lying, she is one hell-of-an-actor."

Julia said, "Pop, I believe her, too. Things are just not adding up. The Fowlers may be back together and are probably faking it. If they are back together, it's only been recently. The police reports show that both of them have had encounters with the Richmond PD as recently as a month ago. The question is, why is Child Services discounting Meg's story?"

Pop said, "Beats the hell out of me. It's the same old story. There have been lots of cases where a child claims about being abused that turns out to be untrue. It's a tough call, either way. I'm glad that I'm not a judge.

That night, Meg lay thinking about everything that has happened since she left home; and the people who came into her life. She had never met people like this; and two of them were cops! Much to her surprise, she likes every one of them. She thought, *"Is this the way real families are? These have been the best days of my life."*

If Meg was sent back, she may be going back home or into the Richmond foster care system. She knew several foster kids and they all hated it. *"Wouldn't it be nice to live with someone like Pop and Julia, and Mrs. Petrowski. "I wish I could stay here; always."*

The next Monday morning, Stacy Andrews of Richmond Child Services and her assistant came and interviewed Pop, Anna, Julia and Meg.

After the interviews, the assistant led Meg to another room and Stacy said, "Megan's story is quite a story. Do you believe her?"

Julia said, "We have no reason not to believe her. She ran away and made it all the way here from Richmond. That tells me that, at fourteen years old, she was really scared."

Stacy said, "Sorry, but I have to be a skeptic. We hear these kinds of stories every day and some are true and some aren't. She can't be returned to Richmond until after the hearing. Since Vallejo is out of my jurisdiction, I can only let her continue staying with Mister Petrowski until, and unless, the judge rules that she be brought back to Richmond. I should also tell you that it may take a while before you hear from us; we are seriously understaffed."

Pop said, "That's fine with me. We are in no hurry."

In the meantime, the record checks Pop had requested were completed. The sergeant said, "We found nothing on the girl but her mom's and dad's record can each fill a book. Jake Fowler has an extensive record for trafficking prostitution, robbery and drug charges; but nothing ever sticks. Edith Fowler's record is also a long one. They must have good lawyers and they are smart enough to leave no direct evidence. Another interesting thing is that Jake has been used as a CI (Confidential Informant) from time to time. One thing is for sure, Jake Fowler is a career criminal."

Pop asked, "What about the mother?"

"Edith Fowler is another story altogether. She is a career hooker. She has had numerous arrests for prostitution and drug possession. She has been an off and on derelict until just recently."

Pop thanked the sergeant and asked that the records be sent to the Vallejo PD.

As Pop and Julia were getting ready to go home, Pop asked, "Have you noticed that Meg is always in her room?"

Julia said, "Yes. Every time I want to talk to her, she is in her room."

Pop said, "Maybe we should just ask her why."

Julia smiled and said, "You sure are a smart one; I'll talk to her when we get home."

After Pop and Julia got home, Meg wasn't around. Pop asked Anna, "Mom, where is Meg?"

"In her room."

Julia asked, "Does she stay in there a lot?"

Anna said, "I don't think she would ever come out if I didn't tell her to come out."

Pop asked, "Don't you think that's odd?"

Anna said, "Yes, I do. As a matter of fact, I've been meaning to talk to you guys about that. That's not normal."

Julia said, "I'll go talk to her."

Julia knocked on Meg's door and said, "It's Julia; may I come in?"

"Yes, ma-am."

Julia went into the room and asked, "May I sit on the bed?"

"Sure."

Julia sat on the side of the bed and said, "I want to ask you something; why do you stay in this room so much? Why don't you come out and talk with us?"

Meg looked surprised and said, "I'm not supposed to be with adults."

Julia never would have expected that answer and asked, "Why not?"

Jake and mom always told me that children were never allowed to be with the adults; and that we should always be seen but not heard. I could never speak to adults in the house."

Julia asked, "Have you always been forced to stay in your room?"

Meg said, "I am allowed to eat at the table and I clean the whole house. Otherwise, I stay in my room."

By now, Julia was boiling mad. *That's imprisonment! That's also cruel and unusual punishment! That poor child; she can never be allowed to go back to those animals!"*

Julia put her arms around Meg and said, "I am so sorry, Meg. Look at me."

Meg turned and looked at Julia. "Meg, listen to me; YOU DON'T HAVE TO STAY IN YOUR ROOM! In fact, we want you with us. When we are together, it's our family time. Everyone of us should spend the time we have at home together. Now, come with me."

Meg didn't know what to think but followed Julia to the kitchen.

Pop said, "Hi kiddo."

"Hi."

Pop, Julia and Meg sat at the kitchen table talking while Anna cooked.

Meg thought, *"This is strange. No cussing, no yelling, no orders and no warnings. Are these folks real? I wonder if I could really ask questions or tell them things?"*

Pop said, "Meg, you are pretty quiet. Don't you have anything to say?"

Meg asked, "Like what?"

Julia said, "Like doesn't questions come to your mind when we talk?"

Pop said, "Sometimes, things just come into my mind about something we are talking about so I express my opinion. Don't you?"

Meg, squirming in her chair, said, "Yes, all the time; but I was never allowed to speak to adults."

Anna said, "Well, I can tell you that my house isn't run that way. Anyone can speak their mind in my home."

Pop said, "That's right. The only thing we don't allow is telling lies."

Meg said, "I would never lie to you?"

Pop said, "Really? It seemed that you told a lot of lies already. First, you lied about who you were. You lied about where you came from; and many more."

Meg lowered her head and began to cry.

Anna said, "Peter, there you go again! You've made her cry again."

Pop said, "I'm sorry, Meg."

Meg said, "Please don't be sorry. I did lie; and I am very sorry. But I want you to know that I am not a liar. I was afraid that I would be sent back to Jake and mom."

Pop said, "I know, sweetheart. Just for the record, every one of us at this table has lied sometimes; and that, sometimes, it's okay to tell a lie. Lying to us about that was justified. I should never have said that. The point I tried to make is that we expect to be truthful to each other and not be afraid of saying what we think."

James Youngblood

Julia said, "Okay, enough of this negative shit. Meg, how as your day before this brute spoiled our talk?"

Pop laughed and said, "Ouch!"

Meg thought, *"These folks sure are nice. Pop actually apologized to me; I can't believe that. Why couldn't they be my family?"*

Meg heard everything Pop said and wanted to believe him. The trouble was that Meg didn't believe that men were like Pop.

The next morning, after Pop and Julia left for work, Anna said, "Meg, we have a rule that everyone contributes to the household and you have to do your part."

Meg's heart started beating fast and thought, *"Contribute to the household? Is she going to make me prostitute? I'll run away first."*

Anna saw the look on Meg's face and remembered her tell that Jake was going to make her contribute to the house by having sex with men. Anna quickly said, "Not like at home. I mean that you will have household chores. You will vacuum the floors and dust. I will clean the kitchen and bathrooms on cleaning days. Every day, you will clean off the table and put the dishes in the dishwasher. Lastly, you keep your room clean and help me wash clothes. Does that sound reasonable?"

"Yes ma-am."

Anna never had to tell Meg to do her chores after that.

7

Pop, Anna and Julia attended Meg's hearing, hoping for the best but expecting the worst.

Jake's lawyer put on a great opening argument and Loretta's rebuttal made a great appeal to keep Meg in the care of Child Services. She pleaded that child abuse had been established without determining who was at fault and argued that the court's first obligation was to protect Meg until Child Services concluded that it was safe to return Meg to her parents. Finally, she petitioned the court to allow Meg to remain in the custody of the Petrowski's in the meantime.

They were thrilled when the judge granted Loretta's petition. After the judge's concluding remarks, Meg hugged Pop, Julia and Anna.

When Pop put his arms around her and hugged her, she got the strangest feeling. She had always felt repulsed by the thought of a man's hands anywhere on her body; but this was different. His hugging her made her feel safe and wanted; and not for her body.

Seeing that display of love infuriated Jake and he stared at Meg with hatred in his eyes.

As Jake and Edith walked past them on the way out of the courtroom, Jake said, "You ain't seen the last of me, you little bitch."

Jakes's lawyer said, "Jake, don't say things like that! You are lucky you aren't in jail. Don't screw things up; I can only do so much for you. Don't make things worse than they already are."

After the Fowlers were out of the courtroom for half an hour, Loretta led them out of the courtroom making sure they wouldn't run into the Fowlers on the way out.

Pop said, "Thank you very much, Loretta, you saved the day."

Loretta said, "You're welcome. Like the man said, you ain't seen the last of him. Pop, he is dangerous; and he is mad as hell."

Pop said, "I agree."

They drove home and Meg was very happy. She asked, "Does this mean I can live with you always?"

Anna said, "No, honey. We only get to keep you for six months. Then, there will be another hearing to decide what happens next."

Meg said, "If the judge sends me back there, I'll just run away again."

Pop didn't doubt Meg and everyone remained silent all the way home.

Later that evening, Meg said, "Goodnight; I think I'll turn in. Julia, will you tuck me in?"

Julia was surprised but said, "Of course I will" and flowed Meg to the bedroom.

Meg said, "I wanted to talk to you alone."

Julia wondered why but said nothing.

Meg said, "Anna told me all about the Petrowski family going back to Poland but I don't know anything about you. Will you tell me about yourself and your family?"

Julia said, "There isn't much to tell but I'll try."

Julia began; "I was born Julia Marie Archer on May 16th, 1936 in Oakland, California to Charles, we call him Chuck, and Cynthia Archer.

I came from a large family; I have two brothers, Sam and Fred and two sisters, Jane and Janet. Sam and Jane were older and Fred and Janet were younger. we were all born less than two years apart. The Archer home always looked like a category five tornado ran through the house every day. Mom never stopped cleaning; it was a seven day a week job; and the house was cluttered before she finished cleaning it. we also had three dogs and two cats to add to the chaos. The litter boxes always smelled and there was animal hair everywhere.

I hated the chaos and clutter and dreamed of the day she would go away to college.

I graduated from San Jose State University, with a degree in Psychology.

Although I found psychology fascinating, I didn't want a career in it. As a student, I began reading mystery novels like The Adventures of Sherlock Holmes and watched TV shows like Murder She Wrote. In the end, I opted to work for the police. After college, I was hired by the San Francisco Police Department in their fledgling Crime Scene Investigation group.

In 1967, I quit my job to go to a new forensic college. Before I graduated, I was hired by the Vallejo, California Police Department as Assistant CSI Detective.

I got married to a man named Andy Carl but it didn't last very long. I am now single and I never want to be married again.

Meg said, "Tell me about him."

Julia said, "One day, I looked up from my desk and there stood the most devilish grin she ever saw. He said, "Hi, sunshine, where do I pick up a CSI report?"

Instead of pointing to the desk, I said, "I'll take you."

We walked across the room and I said, "She will help you."

"Thank you, miss?"

"Detective Archer."

"Well, thank you, detective Archer."

An hour later, my phone rang, "Detective Archer."

"Hello detective Archer, this is detective Andy Carl. Remember me?"

I immediately knew who it was but said, "Sorry, I never heard that name before."

Andy said, "Ah! You fatally stabbed me through the heart."

122

I said, "I'm really sorry about that. I'll go to your funeral if that will make you feel better."

"There you go, you did it again. Have you no mercy?"

This time, I laughed and said, "You must be that clown that was in here about an hour ago."

Andy said, "I was there an hour ago but, believe me, I am not a clown; unless clowns fall in love at first sight."

I thought, *"Oh shit! Here it comes; but he is very cute."*

I said, "I don't believe in love at first sight."

Andy said, "Well, I fell in love with you at first sight."

I asked, "Were you born in Ireland?"

Andy said, "No, why?"

I said, "Because you are so full of blarney."

Andy laughed and said, "I'm glad you have a sense of humor. Seriously, I am very attracted to you and I thought we should have dinner together and see if the feeling is mutual. How about it; one cop to another?"

I surprised myself when I said, "I guess we should find out. When?"

Andy said, "Anytime as long as it's soon; very soon. How about tonight?"

I said, "That's too soon. How about Friday?"

Andy said, "But that's four days from now. I may die if I don't see you before that."

I smiled and said, "Then, I'll send flowers."

"Okay. Maybe you aren't perfect after all; you have a cold heart."
I said, "You'd better watch your mouth; I might stand you up."

Andy said, "You win, what's your address?"

"Do you know Enzo's Sicilian Café?"

"Who doesn't?"

"I'll meet you there at six, Friday night."

That began a whirlwind romance. Andy and I had dinner at least three times a week. I took Andy to my parents for Thanksgiving dinner.

Andy took me outside and I asked, "Andy, what's going on?"

Andy said, "I want to do this today while your family is together."

"Do what?"

Andy opened a small box and said, "I want us to get married and honeymoon in Australia. Will you marry me?"

I said yes before I even thought about it. Andy asked, "Is it okay if we simply elope?"

I dreamed of a big wedding but I said, "That's okay with me. When?"

"How about right away and have Christmas in Sydney?"

"Okay."

The entire family was upset but Andy and I were married by a justice of the peace the following Friday; without any of our families attending.

The wedding bliss was gone by the time the plane landed in Sydney. Andy complained about jet-lag so we stayed at the hotel for three days. All Andy wanted to do was watch sports on TV. One day, I had had enough and said, "I want to get out of this damned hotel room."

Andy said, "The game is almost over; we will go in another half hour."

I asked, "Just what do you like about watching golf? To me, it's like watching paint dry."

Andy said, "It's about appreciating skill and strategy."

I didn't get it and that was a fact; and that's the way our honeymoon went.

After we were married, another thing that really annoyed me was that Andy would take off his clothes and throw them on the floor; just the way my brothers and sisters did. I began to think that I was the odd one. *"Maybe this is normal behavior and I'm the one that's abnormal. All I know is that I don't like it."*

By the time Andy and I were married three months, I was having serious misgivings about the marriage. Now, my life was going to work, coming home and cleaning, while Andy watched sports on TV.

Three more months went by the same as always; except when it came time to do the dishes or clean the house. I would also come home from work and cook. After dinner, Andy would go to the couch and turn on some kind of game. Andy never offered to help with anything; and he still left his clothes on the floor. I had finally had enough; I would do no more cleaning and see how long it took Andy to notice.

Andy's pile of clothes by the bed grew and he only said, "Honey, all my clothes are dirty."

That pissed me off so I also stopped washing the dishes. When there were no clean dishes, Andy said, "Honey, there is no clean dishes."

I said, "Then, you might try washing them. While you are at it, pick up your clothes in the bedroom. They are beginning to stink."

Andy immediately got pissed and said, "That's a woman's job."

My initial reaction was to scream at Andy but I stopped myself. Instead, I went to the living room and turned off the TV.

Andy said, "Hey, why did you do that? I'm watching the game."

I said, "Not right now, you aren't. I'm going to talk and you are going to listen."

Andy looked at me and asked, "What?"

I said, "Andy, I quit."

"What do you mean, quit?"

I said, "I want to have our marriage annulled; right away."

Andy asked, "Just like that?"

I said, "Look, Andy, we don't have a marriage; and we never did. We have absolutely nothing in common. Our lifestyles are complete opposites. I can't, I won't, continue living this way. Let's simply annul our marriage and go our separate ways. I harbor you no ills. The simple truth is that you and I could never be happy together. Have you been happy since we got married?"

"Happy?"

I said, "Neither am I and we should be happy. I was happy when I was alone; now, I'm not."

We finally agreed that it was the best way forward; and we parted on friendly terms.

In less than a month, Andy was living with another woman and I was happy being alone in my new apartment.□

Now, Pop and I work together and we are best friends. Now, that's my story. I told you it wasn't very interesting."

Meg said, "I think it's interesting. Are you and your family as close as you and the Petrowski's?"

Julia was caught off guard with that question and didn't answer right away. Finally, she said, "I am close with my family but I don't see them as much as I see the Petrowski's. That's, mostly, because Pop and I work together every day; then, you came into our lives and I see them, and you, every afternoon and evening."

Meg asked, "Where do they live?"

Julia said, "They all live in Berkeley."

Meg said, "I think I would like to meet them, sometime."

Julia said, "I believe that can be arranged; one of these days."

Meg said, "Thank you for telling me all this. I'll let you go so you can get your sleep."
Julia leaned down, kissed Meg on the forehead and said, "Good night."

Meg lay in bed but couldn't go to sleep. She wondered why Julia and Pop didn't get married; they acted like man and wife. Then, Meg was startled and thought, *"How can they be my mom and dad if they aren't married? This is bad."*

This issue would remain on Meg's mind every day and she came to the realization that her new family wasn't a family! Then, again, she worried that the court would send her back to Jake.

8

Ever since they picked up Meg at that seven eleven, Pop and Julia had spent a lot of time together; on the job and after hours.

On Friday, Pop said, "Julia, how about we spend the weekend at Tahoe?"

Julia said, "I think that would be very nice. I'll see if I can get hotel reservations."

After they got to their room, Pop said, "I'm going to love being away from civilization for a couple of days; we both need it."

That night, back at home, Anna woke with a start. She heard a banging on the front door. She put on her robe and went to the door. She looked through the peep hole and saw Jake Fowler. She said, "Go away! I'm calling the police."

Jake yelled, "I want my daughter; and I want her now!"

Anna locked the dead bolt and ran to get the 16-gauge shotgun that Pop had bought for her.

She went back to the living room where Jake was kicking at the door. Anna yelled, "Go away or I will shoot."

Jake laughed and said, "I'm going to get Meg one way or the other" and kicked the door hard again. When he did, Anna pulled the trigger just as the door burst open. The shotgun went off and she shot the floor in front of the door instead of Jake. After the gun went off, its recoil knocked Anna to the ground and Jake took the gun. He hit the ground with the gun, breaking it in half. As Anna lay on the floor, Meg had come to see what was happening. Jake took Meg by the hand

and said, "You little bitch, you are going home. If you try to resist, you will be very sorry."

Anna called 911 then called the hotel in Tahoe and left a message for Pop.

There was a knock on the hotel door. When Julia opened the door, she saw a message addressed to Pop laying on the floor.

"Pop, you have a message."

After reading the message, Pop said, "You won't believe this. Jake Fowler kidnapped Meg last night."

"He did what?"

"You heard me; she is gone. That son-of-a-bitch took her. So much for a peaceful weekend, huh?"

"I'm so sorry. What are we going to do?"

"File kidnapping charges against Fowler."

Pop and Julia went straight from Tahoe to Richmond and filed a kidnapping charge against Jake Fowler.

Jake was arrested but his lawyer argued that a man can't kidnap his own daughter. The district attorney agreed with Jake's lawyer and the kidnapping charge was dropped. Instead, Jake was charged with violation of a court order; that only resulted in a fine of five-hundred-dollars and a court order to return Meg to child services.

When the police went to the Fowler's house, it was empty. The Fowlers had vanished.

When Pop got the news that Jake had disappeared with Meg, he was furious and panic ran through him. He was afraid of what Jake might do to her but had no clue where to start looking for her; they could have gone anywhere.

Pop asked for a leave of absence so he could work full-time looking for Meg.

Finding Meg was not going to be easy. Jake didn't use credit cards so they could be anywhere and never be traced. In 1988, there was no way to trace people's whereabouts. The only tool Pop had was to send a BOLO (Be on the lookout) to every police department in Northern California, Arizona, Utah, Nevada, Oregon and Washington. He handed out pictures of Jake and Meg stating that they were last seen driving a maroon 1986 Thunderbird.

After two weeks, Pop decided that he would return to work. All he could do now is to wait and hope the BOLO would give him a lead.

One day, Pop received a notice that Jake's Thunderbird had been traded for a white 1988 Chevy Camaro in Oakland.

Pop had another BOLO sent out for the Camaro and waited.

Weeks later, Pop hadn't heard anything. It was August 4th, Meg's fifteenth birthday and Julia was at Pop's house having dinner when the doorbell rang.

Pop answered the door to find Meg standing there with a suitcase. "Hi, can I come in?"

Pop hugged Meg and asked, "How did you get here?"

"I drove dad's car. Is there anywhere to hide it?"

Pop led Meg to the dining room and said, "Hey guys, look what I found."

Anna and Julia jumped up and hugged Meg.

Meg said, "I ran away again. Dad insisted that I prostitute for him so I took his car and some of his money and came here."

Anna said, "It's all right, honey. Have something to eat."

"Thanks, I am starved."

Meanwhile, Pop put the Camaro in the garage and came back inside.

Pop said, "The car is in the garage. Where have you been living?"

"In an apartment in Berkeley. Dad figured no one would be looking for us there."

Julia asked, "Did he force himself on you again?"

Meg said, "He tried but I fought him off. He tried to beat me but I hit him with a frying pan. Then, I got a big butcher knife and told him that I would kill him if he ever tried that again."

Anna asked, "What did he do then?"

"He just said that I wasn't that good of a lay anyway."

Julia said, "That's great. Never let him get close to you again."

Meg said, "I'm sorry but I'm pretty sure he will come here looking for me. If you will help find a place for me to live; I'll go there. I stole a lot of cash from dad."

Pop said, "You'll stay here. How much money did you take?"

"I don't know."

Meg reach in her pocket and brought out a large roll of cash wrapped in a rubber band.

Pop counted ten-thousand-dollars and said, "This is a lot of money. He will surely be coming after this."

141

Meg said, "He won't miss it. He has a lot more at home; he doesn't use banks. I'm sure he doesn't know how much money he has. He has rolls like this hide throughout the house."

Julia said, "I think Meg is right. I'll find her an apartment and rent it in my name; and I'll stay with her."

Pop said, "Julia, you know damned well that's illegal. You can be charged with kidnapping a minor or, at least, abetting a fugitive. I say we just sit tight. If he comes after her here, he will use the legal system."

Julia said, "I hope you are right; what should we do?"

Pop looked at Meg and said, "Meg, I'm sorry but the right thing for you to do is file charges against your dad for attempted rape and forced prostitution. That way, there's a good chance the court may put you back in our care."

Meg said, "Okay."

Anna said, "Okay; now that that is settled, I know that this is someone's birthday. Happy birthday, honey."

Meg said, "I forgot all about it. Thank you."

They quietly celebrated Meg's fifteenth birthday. When it was time to go to bed, Meg said, "This is the best birthday I ever had. I love you guys."

The next morning, Pop took Meg to the police station where she turned herself in and filed criminal charges against her dad. After that, Pop called Loretta and explained everything.

After Loretta got to the police station, she said, "Pop, I think it best that I place Meg in a neutral foster home. I know a nice couple that would take good care of her until this is settled. Meg, is that okay with you?"

"Yes, ma'am; whatever you guys' think is best. I'm not as afraid of Jake as I was. I can take care of myself, now."

Pop said, "I'm sorry, honey; we just don't have a choice. Promise me that, if Jake forces you to have sex with him again, you will run, immediately, to the police station. Tell them that Jake raped you and insist that they have you examined. They can tell if someone recently had sex with you; they just can't say who it was. At least, you will establish that you had sex with someone. Also be sure you tell them that he raped you in your home. In the meantime, Julia and I will do everything we can to get you back."

Meg said, "That's what I want more than anything in the world."

Anna burst into tears and hugged Meg.

Pop said, "Okay, it's time to go."

Loretta and Meg walked to the car and Meg waved goodbye to Pop, Anna and Julia.

The three of them continued waving goodbye until the car was out of sight.

Pop drove Jake's car to Jake's home and parked the car. Julia followed in another car and she and Pop went back to Vallejo.

9

Child Services placed Meg with foster parents, Ralph and Nikki Waddell. The Waddell's lived in North Vallejo; in a low middle-class home and neighborhood and Meg was placed in high school as a freshman (9th grade).

Because Meg was a year behind the other kids her age and she was more physically developed than the other girls in her class. She stood out from the others. Adding to this was Meg's having had such poor attendance. The result was that she was, academically, functioning at the sixth-grade level, at best. She was clearly behind all the other kids in her grade.

Other than her poor academics, Meg was mature and wise way beyond her age. She also had a gift for being liked by other kids; boys and girls alike, flocked to Meg.

Most of the freshmen were intimidated by the older students and Meg was quickly singled out as their friend. Being different, and academically behind, the older kids began calling her, Dummy.

One day, Meg saw a boy being bullied and it was apparent that something was wrong with him. Meg went to him and got between the two of them and said, "Leave him alone!"

The bully, surprised that a girl challenged him went away laughing.

The boy, struggled to say thank you. He was very hard to understand but Meg asked, "What's wrong with you?"

The boy finally got Meg to understand that he had severe MS (Multiple Sclerosis) and his name was Henry Hall.

Henry had trouble keeping his head still and had little use of his left hand; worst was, he didn't talk very well. Lots of the older kids taunted and made fun of him every day. One boy, in particular, was the bully she chased away; his name was Jimmy. That made Meg very mad. One day, she got between Henry and Jimmy again and said, "Leave Henry alone. He's done nothing to you."

Jimmy shoved Meg aside and said, "I'll do anything I want; and you, or anybody else, can't stop me."

Meg, came at Jimmy and hit him in the stomach as hard as she could. Jimmy buckled over in pain and just looked up at Meg.

Meg led Henry away and said, "I'm sorry, Henry. I won't let him bother you anymore."

Henry struggled to say, "Thank you, you are very brave."

After that, Meg began talking to Henry every day and soon learned to understand him. Meg and Henry were always together after that; and the younger kids began hanging around with Meg and Henry.

In school, Meg was really struggling. One day, her English teacher, Miss Mendosa, asked Meg to remain after class.

Meg asked, "Did I do something wrong, Miss Mendosa?"

"No, Meg; I just want to talk to you."

"What about?"

Carmen, said, "I see that you are struggling to learn your lessons."

"Yes, ma'am; it's hard."

Carmen asked, "What are you having trouble with?"

Meg said, "Everything. I missed the eighth grade altogether and a lot of the seventh grade. I haven't learned anything since the sixth grade."

Carmen asked, "How did you make passing grades?"

Meg said, "I don't know. I failed my grades but they passed me to the next grade anyway."

Carmen thought, *"How can this be true? She seems to be intelligent so I'll offer to help her."*

Carmen asked, "Would you like me to help you after school?"

Meg said, "I don't know. My foster parents want me to come straight home after school; and they are very strict."

Carmen asked, "Would you mind if I talked to them?"

"No, ma'am."

The next day, Carmen called Mrs. Waddell, "Mrs. Waddell, this is Meg's English teacher, Carmen Mendosa. Meg is having trouble keeping up; may I come over and talk to you and your husband about Meg's difficulties?"

Mrs. Wadell said, "Okay but that girl is a handful. If you can do anything with her, be my guest."

Carmen asked, "May I ask how she is a handful?"

Mrs. Wadell said, "She is moody and keeps to herself. I can't seem to communicate with her."

Carmen asked, "Is it okay if Meg stays after school every day for a while? I will work with her to help her catch up. Meg seems to be a bright girl but is behind the others. I believe I can get her up to the 9th grade level by the end of the school year."

Mrs. Waddell said, "She is a smart girl. I would like that; and I will do anything to help if you will just tell me what to do."

Carmen said, "That's wonderful. Is tonight okay?"

"Yes."

Carmen thought that if Meg was that far behind in English, she must be behind in everything else. Carmen talked to Meg's math teacher and learned that Meg was far behind in math as well. When Carmen asked the math teacher if she would help Meg, she said, "I just can't take extra time with the students. I have to go home and cook dinner every day; sorry,"

Carmen strongly believed that Meg should work on both math and English; at a minimum. Ideally, she would work on other subjects as well *"Maybe I can help Meg with both English and math to catch her up."*

Carmen was single and dedicated to her students; and Meg certainly needed help.

Carmen began teaching English one day and math the next; five days a week. Plus, she gave Meg homework for the weekends.

Meanwhile, Julia was at Pop's house and they talked about Meg; and wondered how she was doing. Anna said, "Why don't we go see her?"

Pop asked, "Do you really think her foster parents would let us see her?"

Anna said, "I don't see why not. I know it won't do any harm to ask."

Pop said, "Mom, you're right, as usual."

Pop called Ralph Waddell, "Mister, Waddell, this is Peter Petrowski, Meg's former foster parents."

"What can I do for you?"

Pop said, "I was wondering if it would be okay with you and Mrs. Waddell, if my mom and friend come to visit Meg."

Ralph asked, "You were her foster parents?"

Pop said, "Yes, we were her foster parents before you."

Ralph asked, "Why did you give her up?"

Pop said, "We had run-ins with her dad and Child Services thought she should be placed in a different home; otherwise, we would have kept her."

Ralph said, "I will let Meg decide. If she wants to see you, she will call you. If she doesn't call you, it means the answer is no."

Pop said, "Fair enough, thank you."

Later, Ralph said to Meg, "Meg, someone called today and said they would like to visit you. His name is Peter Petrowski."

Meg's heart started beating faster and waited for Ralph to say something else.

Ralph finally asked, "Well; would you like to see him?"

"Oh, yes, sir."

Ralph said, "Then, I suggest you had better call him and tell him it's okay to come."

Meg took the number from Ralph and dialed it.

Anna answered the phone, "This is Anna, who is this?"

"Hi, it's Meg."

"Oh, my Heavens, how are you honey? It sure is good to hear from you."

Meg, eagerly said, "Mister Waddell told me that Pop called and wants to come visit me; will you and Julia come, too."

Anna said, "He sure did. Here's Peter."

Pop took the phone and said, "Hi, pumpkin, how's my girl?"

Meg asked, "Are you really coming to see me?"

"We sure are; if you want us to come?"

"Are you kidding? I can't wait to see you guys. I've missed you terribly. I want to see all of you."

"We've missed you, too. How about we come Saturday?"

"That would be great!"

"See you Saturday, then."

Meg told the Waddell's about the Petrowski's and Julia and how much she loved them and how much she looked forward to seeing them.

When Ralph and Nikki were alone, Ralph said, "That girl seems to really love those folks."

Nikki said, "That all she talks about. It's giving me a complex. There is no chance that you and I will ever take their place. She should be with them."

Ralph said, "Since she seems to love them so much, why did Child Services take her from them?"

Nikki said, "All I know is that those people never treated Meg badly."

Ralph said, "I agree."

Pop, Julia and Anna got to the Waddell's at ten o' clock in the morning. After all the hugs, Ralph whispered to Pop, "May I speak to you alone?"

Pop said, "Sure."

Ralph led Pop to his home office and said, "I don't know if you are aware that we aren't supposed to be doing this."

Pops asked, "Doing what?"

"Allowing you to see Meg."

"Why not?"

Ralph said, "The Child Services woman said that Meg shouldn't see anyone she had contact with before; but that girl seems to love you all. That's why I said it was okay. I'm trusting Meg; and you. I know that she has been badly abused and if you were the one that abused her, she wouldn't want you here."

Pop said, "Ralph, we love Meg. We would have her now but the court insisted that she be placed with someone else. Maybe it's because I am single and my mother lives with me. Also, Julia is my work partner; not a member of my house. If it will make you feel better, Julia and I are CSIs with the Vallejo Police Department" and showed Ralph his badge."

Ralph said, "Boy, that's a relief. That's all I wanted to say."

The two of them went back where the others were and Pop gave Ralph and Nikki a business card and said, "If Meg, or you, ever need anything don't hesitate to call me, mom or Julia; day or night, and we will be here."

Julia gave them each one of her cards.

Pop asked, "May we take all of you to lunch?"

Ralph said, "Thank you but why don't you take Meg? Nikki and I will stay here and let you guys catch up; I think you all will be more comfortable without us being there."

Pop thought, *"That's very thoughtful of Ralph. He must not worry about what Meg tells us; that tells me a lot about them."*

Over lunch, Meg told them all about her grade problems at school, her teacher, Carmen; and Henry.

Pop asked, "How do you like the Waddell's?"

"They are okay but I would rather live with you."

Pop said, "Who knows, maybe, one day you will."

"Really?"

Anna said, "Yes, but it might have to be after you turn eighteen."

Meg asked, "You would want me after I am an adult?"

Anna said, "We want you for the rest of our lives."

Meg immediately broke into tears. After she gathered herself, Meg said, I would so love that."

Before they left the restaurant, Pop said, "Meg, you need to know that Child Services doesn't want us to see you. Thanks to the Waddell's, they let us come anyway. If you want us to come back, you must never tell anyone that you see us."

"I won't."

They stayed at the restaurant for another hour before taking Meg back home. They visited with the Waddell's for a little while and went home.

On the way home, Julia said, "It sure was nice of the Waddell's to let us see Meg."
Anna said, "I don't see why that damned judge wouldn't let us keep her. No one besides us seems to care about Meg's rights, needs and wants; and they claim that they look after her best interest?"

Julia said, "That's a lot of bull shit. They don't give two hoots in hell about Meg's rights."

Back at school, Jimmy continued to try and harass both Henry and Meg but Meg continued to stand her ground. Now, the kids began to heckle Jimmy about being put down by a girl. Finally, one day after being ridiculed by the other kids, Jimmy said, "Bitch, I'm going to kick your ass after school. I'm tired of your shit. I'll kick Henry's ass too."

When the bell rang at 3 o'clock, Meg found Henry and said, "Henry, you stay with me."

Meg and Henry went outside and, just off the school grounds, Jimmy and several of his buddies were waiting. Across the street, a bunch of kids also waited to see what would happen.

As soon as Meg and Henry crossed the street, Jimmy and his buddies came toward them. When they got to them, Jimmy went to Meg and shoved her. Without warning, Meg reached over and grabbed Jimmy's balls and squeezed as hard as she could. Jimmy yelled at the top of his lungs and fell to ground writhing with Meg still squeezing his balls.

Meg said, "If you ever fuck with Henry or me again, I'll bring a knife and cut these off."

Everyone began laughing and all Jimmy could do was to look around at everyone laughing at him. Finally, when Jimmy could get to his feet, he limped away toward his home.

That was the last day Jimmy ever bullied anyone again at that school; and Meg became a school hero.

It was coming up to the holiday break and Carmen said, "Meg, you have come a long way and I want you to forget school until after the holidays."

Meg said, "Miss Mendosa, thank you for everything. I hope you have a very merry Christmas and a happy new year."

"You, too, Meg."

Carmen's tutoring definitely made a big difference and Meg was finally testing at the 9th grade level with passing grades in math and English. Carmen planned to tutor Meg in science and social studies after the holidays.

One of the most important things Carmen taught Meg was how to study. Carmen's effort also gave Meg a desire for learning. With Carmen's tutoring, Meg began making straight A's.

Pop, Julia and Anna continued to visit Meg often and Meg's life began steadily improving.

One day, everything changed. Jake and Edith showed up at the Waddell's with a county sheriff and a court order. The court order was to return Meg to her parents.

Meg refused to go with them and the sheriff had to forcibly put her in the Fowler's car. Once in the car, the sheriff said, "I can't do anything else. She is now in your custody."

The Fowler's got in the car and Meg began kicking the back of her mom's seat and yelling, "I don't want to go with you. I'll run away again."

Jake, having had enough of Meg's outbursts said, "You will stay home if I have to chain you to your bed; and that's after I beat the shit out of you."

After they got home, Jake gripped Meg's arm so tight that it badly bruised her arm; and forced her into the house. Meg said, "I want a glass of water."

Jake let Meg go and she filled a glass with water and slowly sipped the water; all the while, staring at Jake.

Edith said, "Meg, honey, don't provoke your dad; you know what you will get if you don't."

Meg thought, *"Just let that bastard try. I'm not going to take it anymore."*

Meg stood by the counter sipping the water until Jake left the kitchen; he said, "You better listen to your mother."

After Jake left the kitchen, Edith said, "Meg, you can't fight this. If you be nice, he won't beat you. He knows that Child Services is watching us."

Meg said, "Mom, that leopard will never change his spots. He's going to come into my bedroom before the end of the day, and you know it."

As Edith turned and walked away, Meg opened a drawer and took out a steak knife, hid it in her waistband and went to her room.

Sure enough, an hour later, Jake came to Meg's room and said, "All right, young lady, it's time for a little fun. I've missed my girl. Take off your clothes."

Jake took his clothes off and said, "I told you to take off your clothes."

Meg said, "No!"

Jake advanced toward Meg and, when he got close enough to grab her, Meg took out the knife and yelled, "I'll kill you, you son-of-a-bitch, if you ever touch me again."

As she yelled, she stabbed at Jake coming very close to his chest. He jumped back and said, "You little bitch, I'm going to take that knife away from you and beat you within an inch of your life."

He lunged at Meg and she drove the knife deep in his shoulder; leaving the knife in his shoulder.

Jake was bleeding profusely and knew that he needed to go to the emergency room. He left, yelling, "I'll get you, damn you."

Meanwhile, Ralph told Pop what had happened. Pop called Stacy and told her about the court order and asked, "How the hell can a judge do this?"

Stacy said, "I don't know. It makes no sense to me. I'll call Loretta and see what she has to say about it."

Pop looked at Julia and said, "I think you and I both know how it happened; the judge on the take."

Julia said, "It's the only thing that makes sense."

Pop said, "I'm going to call Laura Clawson."

Julia said, "Good idea."

Pop called the attorney, Laura Clawson, and set up a meeting. He and Julia met with Laura and told her the whole story about Meg. When they finished telling the story, Laura said, "I think we should file an appeal. I believe we can get this overturned."

Pop said, "I'm sorry but I don't have that kind of money. Is there any way I can do it myself?"

Laura said, "You have a right to try but, in my opinion, that would be a fool's errand. I'll do it; gratis if you cover the out-of-pocket costs."

Pop said, "Thank you, Laura; I'll be in your debt forever."

"No, you won't. I'm doing this in the name of justice for an abused little girl."

A week later, Laura filed her appeal on the grounds that there was a long-standing allegation of physical and sexual abuse and that no evidence was ever produced that the allegations were false. Since a young girl was possibly placed in harm's way by the court, she should be temporarily retuned to the foster parents pending an appeal.

Pop and Laura, with the help of Loretta, built a strong case, assuming Meg was telling the truth.

The new judge granted the appeal, ordered that Meg be returned to the Waddell's and set a hearing date for three months later.

Pop, Julia, Anna, and Laura were at the Waddell's to meet Meg when Stacy brought her home.

After Stacy left, Meg told them about her stabbing Jake.

Laura asked, "Did you, or Jake, file a police report?"

Meg said, "No ma'am, I didn't; I don't know if Jake did or not."

Laura said, "You must go to the police station and file charges against Jake; immediately."

Pop, Meg, Julia and Laura drove to Richmond where Meg filed charges of attempted rape against Jake and stated that her mother was a witness; but probably a hostile witness because of fear of Jake.

Jake was arrested and immediately made bail.

Back in Vallejo, Laura said, "Pop, let's assume that the judge is corrupt and that Jake has connections inside the police department. Given that it's true, we can't trust anyone there. Building a case in defense of Meg will most likely fail; therefore, we need to build a case against Jake and the judge. That will take a lot of time and effort; not to mention, a monumental challenge."

Pop said, "We'll just do what we have to do."

Laura said, "Okay; the first thing we need is names. Meg, I want you to list every name you know or have ever heard Jake mention."

Meg said, "The only names I know are Jake's prostitutes; and maybe a couple more."

Laura said, "That's okay, honey; give us everything you can remember."

Meg made a list and was surprised that she had 26 prostitutes, two street cops, four of Jake's friends and two other pimps on the list.

Laura said, "Pop, you and Julia talk to all the prostitutes and I will have a private detective friend of mine, talk to the others."

Pop asked, "How much will that cost?"

"Nothing. If we find, and prove, corruption up there, we will have the satisfaction of cleaning it up. It won't cost you anything."

Pop asked, "Why are you doing this?"

Laura said, "For justice."
Julia asked, "What do you know about Judge Capps?"

Laura said, "Nothing. We just have to hope that she is honest."

Pop asked, "What are our chances if she is corrupt?"

Laura said, "If we can build a strong enough case, it won't matter. They will throw Jake under the bus in a heartbeat if we can make them believe that we might expose their side business."

Meg said, "The first girl we should talk to is Juanita Marino. I don't know if she will talk but she has seen Jake beat me several times; and she has seen him have sex with me."

Laura said, "Great! "I'll talk to her myself."

10

For Jake Fowler, this was the last straw. He was furious that Meg was taken away again. He thought, *"It's that goddam cop from Vallejo that's behind all this. I'll teach that bastard that I am not a man to fuck with. Meg belongs to me!"*

Jake was also pissed off at Edith; he came home and found her stoned. After he beat her, he told Juanita to see that Edith sobered up and stayed sober.

Jake had become a lot more abusive to both Edith and Juanita since Meg ran away. He had pulled a lot of strings that he didn't want to pull to get Meg placed back in his custody; now, it was for nothing.

Juanita finally got the nerve to say something to Jake. She asked, "Jake, how can I stop Edith? I know that she won't stay here; you can't make me responsible for her."

Jake slapped Juanita so hard she fell to the ground and said, "You clean her up and keep her clean; if you don't it's your ass."

As Jake was leaving, he said, "I'll be gone for a couple of days; clean this house and Edith better be sober when I get back."

Juanita unlocked the bedroom door and went inside. Edith was sitting on the edge of the bed. Edith looked at Juanita and asked, "Did Jake do that?"

"Yes; and I am getting damned tired of his shit. I am supposed to keep you here and sober or he will take it out on me."

Edith asked, "Why do you stay here?"

Juanita said, "I can't get away from him. He has too many people watching me, including some cops."

Edith said, "Yeah, that's why I stay. I would really like to get myself clean and get away from Richmond; if I could find a way to do it."

Juanita said, "Me, too. If you want to stay clean, why don't you?"

Edith said, "Every time I get into withdrawal, I can't keep from getting drugs. Will you promise to stay with me through my withdrawal? If you will stay with me and keep me from leaving, I might have a chance to get clean; it will only take a few days."

Juanita said, "I promise."

Edith said, "After I get sober, I'll help you get away if you really want to."

Juanita said, "First, I don't have any money; Jake takes most of the money I make. Second, "he has too many ways to track me down wherever I go. You know he has the police on his side; I can't outrun them."

Edith said, "If you can figure out how to get away, I'll give you the money you need to stay away."

Juanita asked, "You really have money?"

Edith said, "No, I know where Jake hides his money. If I can stay clean for a while, I'm going to leave."

Juanita asked, "Why don't we go together? We could lean on each other."

Edith said, "I will if you can think of a way."

Three days later, Jake came home. Juanita was sitting in the living room and Jake asked, "Where is Edith?"

"She is locked in the bedroom. She has been going through withdrawal since you left. I cleaned the house real good; see?"

Jake didn't respond and went to the bedroom and went in. Edith was sitting on the edge of the bed holding her head. Jake said, "You look like shit."

"I feel like shit."

Jake asked, "Are you ready to come out?"

"I need a shower and some coffee."

Jake yelled for Juanita to come. "Stay with Edith while she showers and gets dressed."

After her shower, Edith said, "I feel better, thank you, Juanita."

Juanita said, "Edith, don't provoke Jake. He is in a foul mood."

Edith said, "I'll behave."

Juanita asked, "Are you still of a mind to stay clean?"

Edith said, "Yes, I am; and I need your help for a while."

Juanita said, "I'll be here for as long as you need me."

Edith got a cup of coffee and looked in the fridge for milk; it was empty. She said, "Jake I need to go to the store; there's no food in the house."

Jake said, "Juanita will go; you stay here."

Juanita got in the car and headed for the grocery store. She didn't notice the black sedan pull onto the street and follow her to the store. Juanita pulled into the parking space and the sedan stopped behind her, blocking her in.

A woman got out of the car and asked, "Are you Juanita Morino?"

"Who are you?"

Julia showed her badge and said, "Police. We need to talk to you. Come with me."

Julia put Juanita in the backseat and followed her in. Pop then drove to a café and said, "We can talk here. After we talk, we will take you back to your car."

"What do you want from me? I haven't done anything wrong."

Julia said, "We just want to talk to you."

"About what?"

Pop said, "About Jake and Edith Fowler. Are you still living with them?"

"Yes."

"Of your own free will?"

Juanita didn't answer.

Pop said, "I'll just tell you what we believe. We believe that you are Jake's live-in prostitute and that it is not by your choice. On the assumption that we are correct, we can offer you a definite way out of Jake's house and away from his control. All we ask is for your help. Now, the ball is in your court."

Juanita couldn't believe what just happened. *"A way out? Is he for real?"*

Juanita, hesitatingly, asked, "What would I have to do?"

Pop said, "Cooperate with us to put Jake in prison where he belongs. That would mean giving us information and testifying against him. We can offer you witness protection; you could start over somewhere else under a new name."

Juanita said, "You know that if Jake found out, he would have me killed?"

Julia asked, "Do you really believe Jake would have you killed?"

"Yes, I do."

Pop asked, "Do you know if he has killed anyone?"

Juanita said, "I know that he said he was going to kill people and they were never seen again."

Julia said, "Juanita, we also want to save Meg from Jake and a life of prostitution. She is the real reason we are here; to save her."

Juanita said, "That's a very good girl; and smart. She hates living with Jake and Edith. Jake does terrible things to her and treats her like shit."

Pop asked, "What do you think of Edith?"

Juanita said, "She is just a poor soul; helpless. Jake destroyed her life and keeps her drugged and a prisoner in her own house or forces her on the street. She just went through withdrawal and wants to stay clean. She would leave if she only knew how."

Finally, Pop said, "Okay, Juanita, it's time to fish or cut bait. Will you cooperate?"

After a long moment, Juanita said, "I will cooperate if you take me somewhere away from here right now; this minute. Lock me up for a while if you need to; just get me out of here and I will do anything I can to help."

They left the café and headed north on I-80. Juanita asked, "May I know where we are going?"

Julia said, "We are going to the Vallejo police department. After we question you, we will put you in witness protection in

Vallejo until Jake goes to trial. After the trial, you may go anywhere in the country you want to go; with your new identity."

Juanita was quite for a while and Julia asked, "Are you okay?"
Juanita said, "Actually, I've never felt better. I feel like I am reborn. The question, now, is where do I go and what will I do?"

Pop said, "That's a great way to look at it. This is a new beginning and you can do anything, and be anyone, you like."

Juanita said, "I just know what I'm not going to do anymore. Will you also help Edith get out?"

Julia said, "We will do what we can to help her; if she stays clean and wants our help."

Juanita was questioned for two days. She swore affidavits about Jake's beatings and sexual abuse of both Meg, Edith, seven other young girls and herself. She gave the names of pimps, under-age prostitutes, two known hit men, four cops, two judges and A city councilman.

Juanita was placed in a safe house with 24-hour police protection.

Pop said, "This is a bonanza! This should be enough to prosecute Jake but we need to get affidavits from others plus find hard evidence on as many of these allegations as we can. We have to get hard evidence against the cops, judges and city councilman. Those cases will need to be solid."

Julia asked, "Who the hell can we trust?"

Pop said, "Nobody. I'm thinking that we might have a case for violating Meg's, and the other under-age girl's, civil rights. I'll try to get the FBI to take the case. If they won't take the case, I'll just have to figure out something else. I know an agent, Isaac Giludbeaux, in the Fairfield office; I'll go see him."

Pop talked briefly to Isaac on the phone and set up a meeting in Fairfield.

Pop had copies of everything to give to Isaac. Pop gave him the large stack of documents and said, "This is everything we have so far. Isaac, I'm here because I don't know who I can trust in the Richmond PD or in the judicial system there. If there is anywhere near the corruption that I believe there is, something must be done to break it up; or prove there is no corruption. Either way, someone outside of the Richmond PD must investigate this; that's why I came to you."

Isaac scanned the stuff Pop brought and said, "Pop, this is way above my pay grade. Let me talk to my boss."

Pop waited for almost an hour before Isaac came back with a man and a woman. He introduced the woman as his boss and the man as the station chief.

The station chief asked, "So, you really believe the girl and the prostitute?"

Pop said, "I do; and so, does my partner. The real question, as I see it, is that what if they are telling the truth and we do nothing."

The chief said, "That's the magic key. We have decided to take the case. We will assign two agents who will work undercover; and they will coordinate with only one person. The fewer involved, the better."

Pop said, "Thank you. This is a big relief. We will help in any way we can. I will be your contact here."

Isaac's boss said, "Just so you know, we will cover the same ground you already covered and interrogate your witnesses again."

"No problem; I expected that. Maybe you can get more out of them than we did."
"If we are convinced after that, we will undertake a full investigation and see how much farther the corruption goes. Lastly, this will be conducted strictly undercover."

Pop got back to the police station and told Julia the news. Julia said, "That's great! I feel better now."

Pop said, "This is a secret operation and only you and I know about it. We can't even tell our boss about it until the FBI says it is okay."

Julia looked questioningly and asked, "They think the corruption might extend way up here?"

Pop said, "No; they just operate that way. The fewer in the know, the better. They said, we never know how deep corruption is until they ferret it out."

Back in Richmond, Edith was still sober and Jake was nervous about it. He had never known Edith when she was sober. Making matter worse, Juanita never came back from the store; and he didn't like this.

Juanita disappeared, Meg wasn't afraid of him anymore and Edith was sober and standing up to him. This had never happened before.

Edith prayed every day to have the strength to stay sober. This was the longest she was sober since she first got high. She knew that Jake was going to make her go back on the street to bring in money; plus, she needed to get medical help to stay clean. The question was, how?

Edith got an idea; steal some of Jake's money and tell him she made it prostituting. That would also give her the opportunity to go to a drug clinic.

Jake kept all his money stashed in various places in the house. He had the money bundled in ten-thousand-dollar bundles and five-thousand-dollar bundles; it was hidden in several different places and he was sure that Edith and Juanita didn't know where it was.

Edith took a large bundle and hid it; and she put the small bundle in her purse.

At dinner, Edith said, "I think it's time I started working, don't you?"

Jake said, "You know, I was thinking the same thing. Good idea. Do you want some help?"

"No, I want to try it sober and see how it goes. You know, because of Meg. I want to get her back so I need to stay clean."

"Good thinking, Edith."

Fortunately, Jake never suspected anything. Edith brought home several hundred dollars of his money a day and Jake never suspected anything; he was pleased that Edith was making so much money.

Edith's only worry was about Juanita. She believed that Jake had done something to her but was too afraid to ask questions.

She was pleased that, with the help of the clinic, she wasn't craving drugs to the extent she couldn't control it.

Jake wasn't paying much attention to Edith because he was so preoccupied with getting Meg back home; in fact, he was obsessed with it.

He, proudly, told Stacy Andrews that Edith was still sober and wanted to stay sober forever. He also told Stacy that he had kicked Juanita out of the house; and assured Stacy that he and Edith had changed.

The truth was that Jake didn't want Meg back because he cared for her, it was because they took her from him; it was vengeance.

Pop and Julia were surprised when an FBI agent came and interviewed both of them.

Julia asked, "Why did they interview us?"

Pop said, "Because no one has interviewed us and taken our statement. Our statements are now under oath."

11

Pop was appalled when he got a call from the Waddell's telling him that Jake got a court order to let him visit Meg.

Ralph said, "He is coming to our house next Saturday. Is there anything we can do to stop him?"

Pop said, "Unfortunately, no, if he has a court order. However, I'll come early Saturday morning around seven. Whatever you do, don't let him in your house until I get there. Tell him to come after nine."

Ralph said, "Thank you very much."

Pop told Julia and she said, "I'm coming with you; if it's okay with you."

"Of course, it's okay with me. I wouldn't go without you."

Pop and Julia arrived at the Waddell's at ten minutes after seven. Pop asked, "Have you heard from Jake?"

"He called and said he would be here at eleven and wants to take Meg to lunch. Do we have to let her go with him?"

Pop said, "Absolutely not. He only has visitation rights. Don't worry, I've got this."

Ralph asked, "Do Nikki and I have to be here when he's here?"

Pop said, "Not if you don't want to. Julia and I will stay with Meg."

After Pop and Julia hugged Meg, she asked, "When will I be able to go live with you?"

Pop said, "Honey, we are working on it but it's going to take a while. There are things happening that I can't talk about but we are going to get you back; it's just a matter of time. Unfortunately, we must get Jake put in prison before we can get you back."

Meg shrugged her shoulders and said, "Okay."

Julia asked, "How are the Waddell's treating you?"

"They are great but I want to be with you guys."

Julia said, "One day, you will; I promise."

Ralph came in the room and said, "If you don't mind, Nikki and I will leave until Jake goes home."

Pop said, "Sure, no problem. I'll make sure Jake leaves by five and we can all go to dinner together."

Ralph said, "Why don't you guys go without us. That way, you can have time with Meg. We know that she wants to spend as much time with you as she can."

Julia said, "That's kind of you, thanks."

Jake showed up on schedule and was clearly upset to see Jake and Julia instead of the Waddell's.

Jake asked, "What are you doing here?"

Pop said, "We are here to supervise your visit."

Jake laughed and said, "Sorry. I've got you this time. The court order says that I can take her for six hours. Where is she?"

Jake thrust the court order to Pop and pop said, "That court order doesn't mean a thing to me; it's not enforceable in this county. You will have to have a local court order and a local police officer enforce it. By the time you get that order, I'll take Meg somewhere you can't find her. So, if you truly want to spend time with her, you are welcome to come inside; however, we won't let Meg out of our sight."

Jake got very mad and said, "I'll have your ass for this"; and he stormed out of the house."

Pop yelled, "Meg, you can come out now."

Meg came into the room and asked, "Where's Jake?"

Julia said, "He decided to leave. He wouldn't visit with us in the room."

Meg ran to Julia and hugged her, then to Pop and hugged him. "I love you guys so much. I'll be glad when this is all over."

Jake got home, called judge Langley and said, "I want that bastard, Peter

Petrowski's ass in jail. He defied your court order and wouldn't let me have Meg."

The judge said, "You shouldn't have had the order in the first place. We can't use that as an excuse to have him arrested. Doing that could have a lot of unwanted consequences for both of us so you are going to have to be patient while a case is being made; and it's going to take time.

Don't rock the boat or you will fuck up everything. Sit tight and keep your mouth shut. I know you don't really want to spend time with your daughter; you just want vengeance. Trust me, vengeance will bite you in the ass; and mine if we aren't very careful so don't push me."

"Okay; okay."

That night, Pop, Julia and Meg had a very nice dinner. When they got back to the

Waddell's house, Ralph asked, "Detective, may I talk to you alone for a minute?"
"Sure."

Pop and Ralph walked outside and Ralph said, "Nikki and I can't do this anymore. We really care about Meg but we didn't sign up for all this dangerous stuff. I am afraid of her father; he is a dangerous man. What can I do to have her taken back?"

Pop said, "Just call Loretta and tell her that you want to send her back."

"Will they come get her now? I'm afraid that he will come back for her. In fact, he might be out there watching to see when you leave. Why can't you take her with you and I'll tell Loretta where she is?"

Pop said, "It's highly irregular but I understand where you are coming from. I'll take her tonight. I'll call Loretta in the morning. If Jake is watching, he will see us putting Meg's things in the car and see her leave with us; he won't bother you after that.

I will also have Loretta tell Jake that Meg is back in Child Services care. That should take you out of the picture altogether."

Ralph said, "Thank you so much. I'm sorry we are so afraid; but we are."

"No problem, we understand."

It was after bedtime when they got home and put Meg's things in the house.

The next morning Pop called Loretta and told her what had happened. He said, "I didn't know what else to do so I brought her home with me. I really believe Meg needs to be away from Richmond for a while. Is there any way you could have her transferred to the Vallejo Child Services?"

Loretta asked, "You mean so you can have her?"

Pop, a little bit annoyed, said, "If it makes you feel better, place her with someone else in Vallejo. I just want her to be close enough so I can look out for her. I truly believe Meg is in danger if she is where Jake can get to her."

Loretta said, "I want you to call Stacy and have her come get Meg; right now. You are too much involved to be objective."

Pop said, "Okay, I'll call her right now."

Stacy's phone was busy so Pop hung up. About five minutes later, Pop was about to dial the phone when it rang, "Hi Pop, it's Stacy. I just talked to Loretta; she is transferring Meg to my custody on the condition that you can't have her. Why is she so against you keeping meg?"

Pop said, "I don't know. It makes me wonder if she is involved with Jake and his bunch; or is being paid off, or scared off."

Stacy said, "Since everything about Meg has been unorthodox, I'll do one more unorthodox thing. Since Julia lives at your house and has Anna there to help, I'll place Meg in Julia's care; if she agrees."

Pop said, "She will agree."

Stacy said, "I'll bring the papers for Julia to sign later today; too bad you two aren't married."

Pop asked, "Could we have joint custody?"

Stacy laughed and said, "Nice try but that won't work."

Stacy came to Pop's house and asked Meg, "Do you want to be placed with Julia? For the record, you can say no if you don't want to go with her."

Meg quickly said, "I want to go with her."

Stacy said, "Okay; now, no one should know where you are. I'll go to the school and have them close your records to anyone without a court order; including your current address."

Pop said, "Stacy, just so we are clear; Meg will also be staying here with mom and I."

Stacy said, "Technically, no; she is with Julia. Julia just happens to live in the same house as you do. Legally, Julia is responsible so all I need is her approval. As far as Child Services is concerned, Meg lives with Julia and she can visit with anyone with Julia's okay."

Anna, who has been silent throughout all this, said, "No one could argue against that, could they?"

Stacy said, "No, they couldn't."

Pop said, "I think that is a fantastic idea."

Meg was glad to be back with Pop, Julia and Anna and to be back in school in Vallejo.

Carmen was happy to see Meg again and said, "I think, maybe, you need my help to catch up again, huh?"

"Yes, ma'am; thank you."

12

After Meg went to bed, Julia asked Anna, "Are you sure you want me to stay here for a while?"

Anna said, "Julia, you can move in permanently as far as I am concerned. I love having you here."

Julia looked at Pop and he said, "Hey, the whole world knows that I love you and we have a thing. I think you should move here; there is no reason for you to pay rent for an apartment. Who knows, maybe you might decide to marry me."

Anna asked, "Are you proposing to Julia?"

"Mom, I already have and she won't have me."

Julia, red-faced, said, "Anna, it's not like that. We both decided it would be best not to get married."

Pop said, "She's right, mom, I was kidding."

"Why didn't you tell me that you proposed?"

"Because we agreed to not get married."

Anna said, "Since you aren't married and Meg is in the house, you can't sleep together."

Julia said, "No problem, Anna. That won't happen unless we are married."

A couple of days later, Loretta called and said, "Jake Fowler is an unhappy camper; and I don't appreciate what you and Stacy have done. I'm not the enemy here; I am only looking out for Meg's best interest."

Pop said, Meg needs to be where I can protect her; it's not about you."

Loretta said, "Jake says he knows that you have Meg and he is determined to get her back. Pop, be very careful."

Pop said, "Don't worry. By the way, Julia is moving to our house. Mom invited her to rent one of our rooms."

Loretta said, "That's good to know."

Meg was happy that Julia would be living with them. As far as Meg was concerned, she finally had her dream family; a mom, a dad and a grandmother; even if it wasn't legal.

Meg's only fear was that the court would send her back to Jake; and that he would do something to hurt Pop, Anna or Julia.

Meg believed that Jake had one of his prostitutes killed for skimming money from him and a john that crossed him. She also knew that she had never seen Jake so mad about anything; he simply will not do nothing.

Julia sensed Meg's dark mood and asked, "Honey, what's wrong?"

Meg said, "I'm scared that Jake is going to do something awful. He is very vengeful; and he's been embarrassed."

Pop said, "Don't worry about us; we can take care of ourselves."

In Richmond, Judge Langley sent word for Jake to meet her at Frenchie's Bar & Grill.

The judge said, "Jake, this situation with your daughter has gotten out of control. I just got word that the FBI is investigating you, and possibly me, because I bent a lot of rules for you. I know you want your daughter back but I don't believe it's because you love her; and I know that she isn't your biological daughter. I now have to do what I should have done in the first place; I must take her from your custody, permanently."

Jake said, "Okay, okay."

The judge said, "Now, Jake, I'm going to ask you to do something you aren't going to like. I want you to apologize to your daughter and those detectives that have her. You need to convince them that you only want what's best for Meg."

Jake said, "I don't know if I can do that."

The judge said, "Well, Jake, you had better; or we will all end up in jail. That's the only way the investigation will be called off. You and I both have far too much to lose over an unwanted step-daughter."

Jake said, "You're right, I'll take care of it."

The next day, Jake called Pop, "Detective Petrowski, this is Jake Fowler."

Pop thought, *"Why the hell is he calling me?"*

Pop hesitatingly asked, "What can I do for you?"

"I have some news that I believe will be good news but I have to do it face-to-face; with Meg and Miss Archer there as well. Detective, this is very important for Meg."

To say Pop was suspicious would be a big understatement; but Pop reluctantly said, "Okay."

Jake asked, "Is tonight, okay?"

Pop said, "Not tonight; make it four o'clock this afternoon at the Vallejo PD; I'll have Meg there."

Jake asked, "Will you please have your mother there as well?"

212

Pop thought it was a strange request but he said, "Sure, I can do that."

Anna and Meg got to the police station at four-thirty. Pop arranged for them to meet with Jake in a conference room; and had guards posted inside and outside the door.

To everyone's surprise, both Jake and Edith arrived with Jake pulling a large suitcase on rollers. On top of the suitcase was a medium-size cardboard box and Edith was carrying a small suitcase and a large bouquet of flowers.

A guard said, "I'm sorry but you can't take those things in the conference room. And, we have to search everything?"

Jake said, "Yes, of course; I didn't think."

The guard said, "Go in that room."

Pop, Julia, Anna and Meg were sitting at the far end of a long table and Jake and Edith sat at the other end of the table.

Jake, looking at Meg, said, "First, Meg, I want to apologize for the way I've treated you and I am asking for your forgiveness. Second, I apologize to all of you for the way I have behaved. Third, Meg, your mom and I have waved our parental rights giving Child Services the freedom to place you anywhere they choose. Where you live will now be between you and Child Services.

Lastly, we brought all your things from our house except some worn-out clothes. Your mom and I wish you the very best."

Edith said, "I am so sorry, honey. I hope someday you can find it in your heart to forgive your mother."

Everyone remained silent. Meg looked at Jake, her mother, Pop, Julia and Anna but said nothing. She was too stunned to say anything.

Finally, Pop broke the silence by saying, "Mister Fowler, Mrs. Fowler, you did a good thing today. I promise that we will take very good care of Meg.

Jake said, "Thank you. You will be hearing from Child Services to confirm what I just told you. Now, if you don't have anything more, we will leave."

Pop said, "We have nothing to add."

After the Fowler's left, Meg screamed, "Is it true?"

Pop said, "I'll believe it when I hear from Child Services. Now, let's get your things and go home."

They got home and took Meg's things to her room. Meg ruffled through the cardboard box until she found the locket.

She said, "My grandmother gave this to me when I was a baby. I don't want anything else. I want nothing that will remind me of them or my life before you took me in."

Pop said, "Okay, I'll trash it."

The next day, Child Services called Pop to confirm that he could have full custody of Meg; and that he and Anna needed to come to Richmond and sign more custody papers.

The next day was Saturday and Julia said, "Meg, you, Pop and I are going shopping."

They spent all morning buying Meg a complete wardrobe of nice clothes, shoes and accessories. Meg felt like a princess.

In the meantime, Jake was fuming about having to humble himself to Meg and those damned detectives. He racked his brain to think of who tipped off the FBI;

he finally decided that it must have been Edith. He figured that she did it after she sobered. Jake confronted Edith but she denied saying anything to anybody; Jake didn't buy it. Jake beat Edith but she still denied saying anything. Not convinced, Jake injected heroin into Edith's arm and kept her drugged for days; long enough that she was hooked again. Once Edith was hooked, Jake threw her back on the street and saw to it that she was kept drugged.

A month later, to Jake's surprise, Edith was trying to get sober again. He was determined that Edith stayed stoned. He, furiously, injected Edith with a much larger shot of heroin and she died from the overdose.

Because of Edith's drug history, the police report stated "Accidental death by overdose of Heroin". Jake was never even suspected; he had gotten away with murder; again.

After they heard the news of Edith's death, Meg said, "I'm sorry but I don't have any feelings for her; she never was a mom to me. Am I a bad person for not feeling sad?"

Julia said, "No. Like you said, she only gave birth to you, didn't know who your father was and never took care of you. Mothers have to earn the title Mother; Edith didn't."

Meg said, "You have already been more of a mother to me than she ever was. I love you and I never loved her."

Pop and Anna were officially named Meg's foster parents and Meg was happy for the first time in her life. She had a new family; and Miss Mendosa.

Meg soon began imagining what her life was going to be like. Pop and Julia told her that she could be anything she wanted to be or do anything she wanted to do; and she now believed them.

After a short time, Meg asked Julia, "Do you think I could become a nurse?"

Julia said, "Honey, you can become a doctor if you want."
Meg said, "I want to be a nurse."

Julia asked, "Why not a doctor?"

Meg said, "It would take too long. I can help people as a nurse and do it a lot sooner."

Julia said, "Then, nursing school it is but you better tell Pop; he has to pay for it."

Meg said, "I forgot about that. What if he won't?"

Julia said, "He'll pay, but if he won't I will. You will go to nursing school. All you need to do is make good grades all through high school."

Meg said, "I can make good grades if Carmen will help me."

Julia said, "I can also help; and I would like to do that."

13

The first thing Meg did after she got to school was look for Henry and he was really happy when he saw Meg.

Henry had been lost after Meg went back to Richmond but, at least, he hadn't been bullied and had friends.

Changing schools set Meg back again and she needed a tutor in more than English and math; she needed to add social studies. Anna decided to talk to Carmen.

After school let out for the day, Meg ran to Carmen's room, opened the door and said, "Hi."

"Oh, my goodness! Hi. It's good to see you?"

Meg excitedly said, "I am back here again; in school. I have been permanently given to Pop and Anna; Pop is, officially, my dad."

Carmen said, "I'm very happy for you, Meg; welcome back."

Meg said, "I am also here to ask you for a very big favor; will you tutor me again. I need help to catch up again plus I need help in social studies. Will you please help me?"

Carmen told Anna that she couldn't give any more time to tutor Meg in social studies; but she would give Anna some teaching material and together they might be able to give Meg what she needed to pass her course.

Carmen really cared for Meg and she enjoyed having something meaningful to do in her off hours.

Carmen set up a two hour a day schedule for the three subjects. It was, basically, a nothing more than a rigorous homework routine where Anna helped by explaining how to do the homework.

Anna and Carmen soon discovered that Meg had a major reading problem; and that this was the cause of most of her learning problems.

Carmen said, "Mrs. Petrowski, I don't know how I didn't see this problem before. I think we should change our routine. Let's make Mondays for math, Tuesdays for English, Wednesdays for social studies and Thursdays and Fridays for simply reading. We'll begin with simple books and let her proceed at her own pace. I'll help with reading comprehension. Most important is that if she likes what she reads, and understands what she is reading; hopefully, she will learn to like reading."

Carmen brought the book, "Lassie Come Home" and said, "Meg, I think you might like this book. I want you to read it, and if you like it, I'll get you another after you read this one."

Meg reluctantly took the book and looked at the cover; there was a picture of a beautiful dog and little boy. Meg was immediately captivated by the picture; however, she wasn't thrilled about having to read a book.

By the time Meg finished chapter one, she was hooked. She took the book to bed with her and read until she fell asleep.

The next day, Meg couldn't wait to continue reading the book; she finished the book at nine-thirty that night.

Meg told Carmen how much she liked the book and Carmen said, "I think you might like this one next" and gave the book to Meg. It was "Call of the Wild" by Jack London.

When Meg gave that book back to Carmen, Carmen said, "This one is very different but I think you might like this as well. It's "The Diary of Anne Frank". When you finish this one, I want you to write a synopsis of each book and each synopsis must contain a minimum of 250 words and not more than 500 words."

Meg wasn't thrilled about writing the synopses but she looked forward to reading the book.

Those books had captured Meg's soul and she was surprised at how easy writing the synopses were.

Meg found herself relating to Anne's story even though their lives were far different; Meg had many of the same fears that Anne had.

After she finished the book, she began reading it again; this time letting her imagination carry her back to the little room with Anne. The book took Meg to another world and time. The first two books were a pleasure to read but this one moved Meg deeply. From that moment on, Meg became a voracious reader.

Carmen, next selected a variety of classics to both stimulate Meg and teach her about other lives, times and experiences.

After a while, Meg began to better comprehend all her school subjects and all her grades improved dramatically.

In the meantime, Meg asked Pop if she could invite Henry to dinner. Pop was surprised; and was immediately worried. *"Bring a boy home for dinner? I don't like this; at all! she is only fifteen. I guess it comes with being a parent."*

Pop said, "Sure"; *"At least, she wants to bring him home."*

Meg said, "Thanks Pop" and ran over and gave him a hug.

Anna saw the look on Pop's face and later, when they were alone, said, "Peter, this isn't what you think it is. Henry has severe MS and she is his best friend."

Pop said, "Then, I think we should invite his parents as well."

Anna said, "That would be a very nice thing to do. I'm sure they would want to know something about us before agreeing to let Henry to come alone for the first time. Most people can't deal with someone with MS."

The next morning, Pop said, "Meg, I want you to ask for Henry's phone number. I want to invite them to come with Henry."

Meg said, "That would be great! I have their number."

Pop called the Hall's number, "Mrs. Hall?"

"Yes."

"Mrs. Hall, I am the foster father of Meg Fowler."

Before Pop could say another word, Mrs. Hall said, "Please call me Frances. I want to tell you that Meg is an angel. She is the only friend Henry ever had."

When Frances caught her breath, Pop said, "I am calling to invite you folks to dinner at our house. Meg wants Henry to come here for dinner, and for regular visits after school or on weekends. I felt that we, all of us, should meet first. We would love for you to have dinner with us and get acquainted."

Frances said, "I agree; we would like to meet you but dinner might not be a good idea. Henry's condition causes him to make a mess when he eats."

Pop said, "If he can eat at home, he can eat here. I assure you that it won't bother us."

They decided on having lunch on Saturday instead of dinner. When Anna was setting the table, Frances said, "I always put Henry at one end of the table so he is less likely to get food on anyone. People are always very uncomfortable being around Henry, especially when he eats; he also will not let anyone feed him. The result is; he makes a big mess at the table."

Anna said, "That's no problem. We will just let him do what he does at home. I'll assure you that we won't be uncomfortable."

Frances said, "Bless you. I have a small blanket that we can put under his chair."

When they all sat down, Frances put a large apron on Henry; one that wrapped around him; and said," Now, we are ready for battle."

Meg sat next to Henry and asked him what he wanted on his plate. Henry told her; and when his plate was filled, he said, "Thank you, Meg." Only Henry's parents and Meg understood him.

It was obvious that Henry was very nervous and he was a lot more animated than usual. He simply couldn't get food in his mouth. Meg, gently, put her hand on his left arm and Henry immediately settled down. Further, as long as Meg's hand was on his arm, he remained calm and fed himself without making a mess.

Frances and Harold watched in amazement as Henry ate with little trouble.

After eating, Meg took Henry to her room to read to him.

After they were out of the room, Harold said, "I have never seen Henry like this."

Julia said, "I think Meg's touch calms Henry. Eating in front of people is probably traumatic for Henry so he focusses his mind on Meg instead of us."
Frances said, "Another thing about Meg is that she understands Henry, maybe better that Harold and I; I believe that girl is gifted."

Pop told them that he and Julia were CSI detectives and his mom was retired. Anna quickly said, "Temporarily retired. I plan to go back to work after Meg goes to college."

Harold said, "I am a cabinet maker and Frances is a homemaker and caretaker for Henry."

They talked until it was nearing time to go and Harold said, "I want to thank you folks for having us. This is the first time we have shared a meal with someone in more than fifteen years."

Pop said, "I think we should do this frequently."

Frances said, "I would love that. Maybe we can alternate hosting the other."
Pop asked, "Does Henry like pizza?"

Frances said, "He loves it. We have it delivered all the time."

Pop said, "I think we should treat the kids to pizza; at the pizza place."

Harold said, "I don't know. It might turn into a disaster."

Julia said, "It won't be a disaster. I believe Henry would like that very much; especially if Meg is with him."

Harold said, "I'm game, if you are."

Pop, Anna, Julia and Meg had dinner at the Hall's and, following that, went to the pizza place. Henry was thrilled, and with Meg's calming effect, did very well.

One day, Meg got to school and looked for Henry. To her shock, she saw a guy talking to Henry. She walked up to them and Henry said, "This is my new friend, Bill Foster."

Meg said, "Hi."

Bill blurted, "You can't be Henry's friend."

Meg asked, "Why not?"

"Because you're normal and he isn't."

Meg said, "Well, Bill Foster, I am Henry's best friend. When did you become his friend?"

"Right now."

Meg asked, "Why?"

"Because Herny is weird like me; but different. I have Asperger's."

Meg asked, "What's that?"

"A disorder."

The questioning went on for a while and Bill never told her what Asperger's was. As far as she was concerned, it meant that he was very rude. The three of them parted ways and went to their respective rooms.

That night, Meg asked, to no one in particular, what is Asperger's?"

Anna said, "I don't know."

Pop said, "I don't have a clue."

Julia said, "It's a mental condition. I could tell you but I think you should look it up at the library."

The next day, Meg, Henry and Bill talked before class. As always, Bill just turned and left without a word. Meg shouted after him, "See you, Bill."

Meg got a book about Asperger's Syndrome, and with Julia's help, read the entire book. Over the next couple of months, Meg read more books about Asperger behavior; it helped Meg better understand Bill's behavior. He wasn't trying to be rude; it was a symptom of Asperger's.

One day after school, Meg, Henry and Bill were talking when Bill's mother, Shirley, walked up to them and said, "Hello".

Bill said, "These are my friends, Henry and Meg."

Shirley asked, "Friends?"

Bill said, "Yes; I told you I had friends."

Shirley said, "I am very happy to meet you."

Bill said, "Bye" and walked away leaving Shirley standing there. She said, "I'd better get going, bye."

That night, Shirley couldn't wait until Jim got home. When he got home, Shirley said, "You will never guess what I witnessed today."

Jim said, "Why don't you just tell me."

"Bill has two friends!"

"What?"

"Bill has two actual friends. One is a girl named Meg; she is normal, and Henry who has MS. Bill was actually talking to them."

Jim said, "I don't believe it. Are you sure they are friends?"

"That's what Bill and Meg said. I couldn't understand Henry but I think he said they were."

Jim said, "I'll come home early; I want to see this for myself."

Jim and Shirley watched Bill, Henry and Meg from a distance and saw that Bill was actually talking to them. Jim said, "You're right. I wouldn't have believed it if I didn't see it. Let's go meet them."

Jim met Meg and Henry and just stood silent while the three kids talked until Frances came to get Henry. She talked to the Fosters for a few minutes and they all left.

At home, Jim said, "I don't get it. Bill never talked to anyone; now two friends? One normal and the other challenged?"

Jim called Bill to the living room and asked, "Would you like for your new friends to come for a visit?"

Bill said, "Yes" and turned around and went back to his room."

237

Jim said, "This is amazing. Let's find out who their parents are and pay them a visit."

The next afternoon, Meg asked, "Would you mind if we invited Bill to our house to study with Henry and I?"

Shirley asked, "You would do that? Bill can sometimes be a problem."

Frances laughed and said, "So can Henry, believe me. It will be just fine."

The first afternoon Bill was there, everything was fine. The next day, Meg said, "Okay guys, today, we will do math first because Henry has a test tomorrow."

Bill immediately got very angry and said, "No! You promised that we would do English first."

Meg said, "Bill, Henry has a test tomorrow so we need to study math today."

"But you said we would do English! I want to go home; now! Bill stamped his feet and started screaming at the top of his lungs. Anna called Shirley, told her what was happening and Shirley said, "I'll come right away. Try to ignore Bill, please. It's the Asperger's. I'm sorry."

Meg tried to calm Bill but nothing she did worked; it only made things worse. Bill was definitely out of control; demanding that they take him home.

Shirley got there in minutes. Bill, stomping his foot, yelled, "I want to go home; now!"

Shirley stood in front of Bill and calmly asked, "Bill, do you want to ever come back here again?"

Bill remained silent for a couple of seconds; then, screamed, "I want to go home, now!"

Again, Shirley very calmly, asked, "Bill do you ever want to come back to visit Meg?"

Bill screamed, "I want to go, now!"

Shirley said, "If you ever want to come see Meg or Henry again, you must apologize right now."

Bill's whole demeanor changed as quickly as it started and he said, "I'll stay."

Shirley said, "Bill, you acted badly; therefore, you have to leave. If you ever want to see them again, apologize right this minute."

Bill said, "I'm sorry."

Shirley said, "I'm very sorry, I really hoped that Meg's influence on Bill would make him behave better."

Bill stormed to their car and Shirley said, "I won't impose him on you again."

Anna said, "Shirley, you weren't imposing. We want Bill to come again; maybe you could teach us how to work with Bill."

Shirley asked, "You would be willing to do that?"

Anna said, "Of course we would."

Shirley said, "I would love that. Bill has shown a lot of progress after becoming friends with Meg and Henry. I think that would help Bill a lot."

Anna said, "Bill, and you, are welcome here anytime."

Shirley arranged to have Bill's therapist work with Meg and Anna to help them understand Asperger's and learn techniques to control Bill's behavior.

One of the most important things they learned about controlling Bill's behavior was to bribe him. Bribery, mixed with a lot of patience, almost always worked. The treats didn't have to be much and, mostly, it was to offer to let Bill do something he wants, likes or wants to go.

Meg quickly became a master at calming Bill and getting him to do what she wanted; even better than his parents.

Meg quickly learned that offering Bill a treat was the only thing that would get his mind off the issue at hand.

As time passed, Meg's study sessions became more structured and Frances got very good at teaching; what's more, she loved doing it.

14

The FBI investigation was stalled and going nowhere; largely, because the FBI wasn't able to have anyone inside the Richmond PD.

Agent Giludbeaux had to think of something; then, he got an idea. He called the Vallejo Chief of Police, Gore, and said, "Chief, we are going to be working on undercover cases in the Richmond area and I would like to meet with you about them; we don't want to operate without coordinating with you, personally. The investigation is top secret so no one should know we are talking."

Louis said, "I would be happy to meet with you."

They set a time, date and place.

When they met, Isaac made up a story about two intra-state crime rings and said, "I need someone to work inside the Richmond PD. Would you be willing to loan Julia Archer to them?"

The chief said, "Not unless I know more about this; like why aren't you talking to the Richmond chief?"

Isaac said, "All I can tell you is that someone inside Richmond PD is believed to be working with our suspects. If that's true, we can't trust anyone there until we clear this up. I can't say more."

The chief said, "Okay but you need to convince the Richmond chief that you have need for an ongoing SCI for a limited time; say thirty to sixty days. I can't just call him and ask him to let her go there."

Isaac said, "No problem; and thanks. I'll get right on it."

Isacc called Chief of the Richmond PD, Carson Sewell, and said, "Chief, this is FBI agent Isaac Giludbeaux of the Fairfield office. I have a couple of cases that we believe have connections in your area. May I come and confidentially discuss these cases with you; I don't want to be operating undercover in your jurisdiction without coordinating with you, personally."

Carson said, "Come any time. My office will help anyway we can."

"Thanks, Chief. I can be there around mid-morning tomorrow if that's not too inconvenient."

"That will be fine."

The next day, in Chief Sewell's office, Isaac said, "We think an intra-state crime organization is trying to set up turfs in Sacramento, Richmond, and Oakland. They are trafficking drugs, cars, and young boys and girls.

My guys and I will be operating undercover and need someone in your office to secretly work crime scenes for us. I have spoken to Chief Gore in Vallejo PD and he can loan one of his CSI agents, Julia Archer, for a month or two. Do you think you could accommodate us for a while?"

Carson asked, "I know her; we use her and her partner on occasion. How do you want to explain what she is working on?"

Isaac said, "Just say that she will be searching for evidence that ties some of her cases to Richmond. Actually, she won't be busy with us full time so you can use her to work on some of your real cases. If you would do this, it would be a perfect setup for us; you get free help and help us at the same time."

Carson said, "Sounds like a deal made in Heaven. I can certainly do that."

Isaac asked, "Is it possible to give her a private office? Since we don't want to be seen in your office, a private office would allow her to communicate with us without being overheard."

"I can do that."

"Thank you very much, Chief. I'll let detective Archer and Chief Gore know that we have your cooperation."

Julia checked in with Chief Sewell and set up her desk. After she was finished, Chief Sewell introduced Julia to the staff and said, "Julia will be coming to some of our most serious crime scenes. Her time will be limited and she will only be here for a couple of months so I want to sign off on all her assignments. I am trying to justify having our own SCI group and Julia can help us do that."

At the chief's staff meeting, Julia said, "If any of you have any questions about SCI, please feel free to ask me. The first thing I want to say is that when an officer first comes on a crime scene, he, or she, must keep everyone away from the area surrounding the scene; in the case of a house, store or building, threat the entire facility as a crime scene. Next, never touch or move anything unless it is absolutely necessary; and always use gloves and take before and after pictures. We don't want your prints to be on anything or the evidence compromised."

Julia was satisfied that no one seemed to suspect why she was there. Working actual crime scenes would be a great cover and give her the opportunity to watch, and interact with, everyone; and get to know them. It was the perfect setup for a mole.

One of the FBI's priority actions was to have Julia go through Jake's house and process it for evidence and information. In order to do that, the FBI had Jake meet with a couple of agents on the basis that they would like Jake to help them on a drug distribution case they were working on. That really peaked Jake's interest. He believed that he could make sure he steered the FBI away from his operation.

While the FBI agents talked to Jake, Julia did a thorough search of Jake's house and grounds. There wasn't much new information found but Julia counted two-hundred-thirty-six-thousand dollars in cash. She took pictures of a couple of bills in each roll so the FBI could trace the serial numbers in case some of it was stolen money.

After looking at everything Julia only found two names that they didn't already have. One was a known petty criminal but the other was found to be a successful building contractor named, Neal Symonoski.

Julia told Isaac, "Isaac, this guy, Symonoski, sticks out like a sore thumb.

There is no legitimate reason for his name to be in Jake's house."

Isaac said, "You're right. He's probably a liaison between Jake and someone else; maybe in the police department. This could be a break we need. Good work."

A couple of weeks later, Deputy Chief, Ray Tosen, went to the Chief's office and said, "Chief, I think we may have a problem. Something fishy is going on with that CSI detective."

The chief asked, "With Julia?"

"Yes. I hear from one of our CIs (Confidential Informant) that she was seen talking to a possible cop or PI (Private Investigator). Is there something going on that I don't know about?"

Carson knew that he had to tell Ray something but not the real reason she was here. He said, "She was talking to an FBI agent. The FBI asked me to let Julia work a couple of undercover crime scenes and didn't want anyone else to know they were working in Richmond. It's some kind of intra-state criminal activity; big corporation stuff, I think."

Ray thought, *"Maybe; but it smells. I'd better put someone on her to be sure."*

Ray also told his administrator, Bridget Stroup, to keep an eye on Julia while she was in the office and had one of his undercover guys, Dale Sweeny, to tail Julia everywhere she went outside the office.

A week later, Bridget reported that Julia asked a lot of probing questions of almost everyone here.

Dale reported that Julia had dinner with the same guy every night; but, other than that, everything looked normal. Dale added, "It's probably just her boyfriend."

Ray thought, *"Why the questions? I can't believe that she and a boyfriend would have dinner together every night and not go somewhere else; like his apartment or a motel. Something definitely isn't kosher about this whole matter. I'd better alert everyone that we might be the target of an FBI investigation."*

Ray spread the word to his people to lay low and cover their asses.

The next night at Julia's dinner with Isaac, Isaac said, "The people we've been watching suddenly changed their daily routines; all at once. I believe that means they might be on to us. The only link we've found is one between Jake and an undercover cop named Dale Sweeny; but we don't have any evidence to prove that there is anything illegal going on."

Julia said, "I haven't found anything suspicious inside."

Isaac said, "We are stopping the investigation. I suggest that you end your stay in a couple of weeks. Just complete the crime scenes you are currently working and don't take on any more."

After Ray cautioned everyone, Jake assumed that someone had been investigating him and he was furious; he thought, *"It's those damned detectives from Vallejo!"*

Julia returned home ten days later and told Pop that she and the FBI couldn't connect the dots between Jake and the police; but she said, "My gut still tells me that someone in the Richmond PD is working with Jake's organization."

Pop said, "That's for sure; we know, for a fact, that someone inside the PD warned Jake. We have to give them credit for being smart. Additionally, the simultaneous change of behavior must have been because of a warning sent out; and my guess is that it was from within the PD headquarters."

Julia said, "If that's true, we must have gotten very close to them."

Pop said, "Bingo!"

Julia said, "I must have screwed up. The only thing I can think of is that I raised a suspicion with my questions and someone must have been watching me. If they were watching me, they would have seen that I had dinner with Isaac every night to coordinate our efforts. That would definitely have had to come from inside headquarters."

Pop asked, "Do you believe Chief Sewell can be trusted?"

Julia said, "If he isn't, he is an Oscar winning actor."

Pop said, "Call Isaac and ask him to come for a meeting with us. I'm not yet ready to throw in the towel."

Isaac came and Pop said, "Isaac, from my perspective, looking at this from outside the box, we all believe that someone inside the Richmond PD is involved with at least one crime organization; we just haven't found any hard evidence. Is that a fair statement?"

Isaac said, "Yes."

Pop asked, "What do we have to lose by bringing Chief Sewell into the investigation and letting him pick up the ball?"

Isaac said, "Nothing. I think that's a good idea."

Pop said, "Okay; Julia and I can't contribute anything more so I suggest that you keep the case open and enlist Chief Sewell. He has been there for thirty-five years. If he is clean, he would know who he can trust; let him conduct an investigation. That way, we have nothing to lose and everything to gain. At a minimum, Chief Sewell will be alerted to the possibility that he has corruption in the department. If he is involved, it might scare him off; that way, we would have accomplished a lot. Either way, we win. Let's hope that the Chief is honorable. If he is, I'm confident that he will eventually rout them out."

Isaac agreed and left.

Two months later, Pop and Julia were watching the evening news when the District Attorney announced that the Richmond PD uncovered inappropriate conduct inside the PD. He said that Deputy Chief Ray Tosen and fourteen others in the police department have resigned; but no criminal charges were filed.

Two days later, Jake Fowler was found dead in his car. He had been shot in the head and a nine-millimeter pistol was found on the car seat; it appeared to be suicide but nobody believed it.

Three months later, Chief Sewell called Pop and said, "I've got some very good news for Megan. Jake had 186 thousand dollars in cash hidden in his house. As his only next of kin, it all goes to Megan. We know it's dirty money but can't prove it. At least, it will go to a worthy cause. Since you are her legal guardian, you can come to Richmond and pick up the money; I want to close this case."

Pop said, "We'll be there tomorrow."

When Meg was told about the money, she had no reaction. Pop said, "Meg, I am going to set up a trust for you so the money will pay for you to go to college. Does that sound okay to you?"

Meg said, "It's okay; but what if I don't want to go to college?"

Pop was surprised and said, "Meg, honey, you have to go to college."

Meg said, "I was thinking of going to nursing school instead of college."

Pop said, "No need to think about that now; college or nursing school is two years from now. The money will be there to pay for whichever you decide at that time."

A few days later, the doorbell rang. Anna opened the door and a tough-looking man asked, "Does Megan Fowler live here?"

Anna said, "Just a moment, please."

She closed the door and said, "Peter, there's a man at the door asking for Meg. He looks like a gangster."

Pop went to the door and asked, "Who are you, and what do you want with Meg?"

"My name is Todd Meunier. I am Megan's biological father and I want to see her."

Pop said, "You will need a court order to even look at her. Her mother swore that she didn't know who the father was so, leave and don't come back without a court order."

Pop told Meg about the man and she said, "I never heard of him."

Julia said, "Meg, he would have to prove that he was your dad; and that can't be proved. He probably knew Jake and knew that Jake kept large amounts of cash; and wants it."

Meg said, "Pop won't let him get any of it."

Anna said, "Well, I can tell you one thing, for sure, Meg certainly doesn't look anything like that man."

The next day, Pop ran a check on Todd Meunier; he had a long criminal record, including an outstanding warrant for his arrest on a charge of manslaughter.

Pop informed the Richmond PD that Todd had been here looking for Meg.

Anna asked, "Hasn't that child been through enough? Maybe we should move and keep our new address a secret until this mess blows over."

Pop said, "Actually, mom, I've been thinking about getting larger house; and in a better neighborhood. Do you really want to move?"

Julia asked, "What about school?"

Pop said, "I wouldn't move before the end of the school year. That gives us plenty of time to find the right house and neighborhood. Is this okay with you, Julia?"

"Are you asking me to live with you in the new house?"

Pop said, "I don't want you to ever not live in my house; it's your home."

Anna thought, *"Why the hell don't they get married? This is crazy."*
A week later, Todd was arrested; they found him watching Pop's house.

Meg would never know the truth but she truly believed that he wasn't her father.

14

Meg, Henry and Bill were inseparable and Bill's social skills had dramatically improved. The three families also became close friends. Meg, Julia and Anna continued to tutor the kids and the three families continued their involvement.

One day, Meg was called to the principal's office. The principal said, "Meg, I would like you to meet Gloria Wade. Gloria, this is Meg Fowler."

It was obvious to Meg that Gloria had a problem.

The principal said, "Gloria is new here and she has no one to show her around or be her friend; will you show her around the school?"

Meg said, "Yes, ma'am."

The principal said, "I am putting Gloria in all your classes so it will be easier for you. Do you think that you could let Gloria join your little study group? It would help her a lot."

"Yes, ma'am; no problem if it's okay with her folks. My dad won't let me have anyone come until he meets their folks; and they agree to be involved."

The principal set up a meeting between Gloria's parents, Ted and Janet, and Pop.

When they met, Ted said, "I want to thank you for inviting Gloria."

Pop said, "You are welcome. It will be a pleasure having her."

Ted said, "Just so you know, Gloria has Autism. It's a milder variation but she has trouble socializing with people. We also think she has attention deficit issues that adversely affects her grades. Mrs. DeGraff told us that your daughter tutors special needs kids; and that you might consider letting Gloria join your study group."

Pop said, "There's always room for one more; however, we have a condition that at least one parent must attend, and participate at all times."

Ted said, "I'm afraid that might be an issue. We both work a lot of crazy hours."

Pop said, "Julia and I both work for the Vallejo PD and work crazy hours. We all work as a team and that guarantees that some of us will always be here to help. We also study on weekends. Maybe you could help then. Having said that, it's your call; however, our condition must stand and I'm sorry if Gloria can't join us."

Ted said, "I understand."

At school, Gloria quickly fit in with Henry and Bill; Henry and Gloria instantly liked each other.

A couple of weeks later, Ted called Pop and said, "Mister Petrowski, my wife and I have figured a way to have at least one of us be there to help. Would that be enough to let us join your group?"

Pop said, "Of course. All we ask is that you and/or your wife take an active part. Some of the things you can also do at home. We just need one of you to be here with Gloria at all times."

Ted said, "Thank you. When can we start?"

Pop said, "There's no time like tonight."

Just like that, the Wade's became a member of Meg's little group.

Pop had been giving a lot of thought about Meg's apparent gift for working with kids with special needs. The group now had three kids; the last was at the request of the school principal.

265

Pop said, "Julia, Mrs. DeGraff must see Meg's gift because she sent Gloria to us. I've been thinking that we should buy a larger house and set up a classroom; do it right and have our own library aimed at special needs kids. Meg, clearly, has a gift; and so, do you."

Julia asked, "I have a gift? No, I don't."

Pop said, "Maybe you weren't born with a gift but your education in psychology and your love for kids, amounts to the same thing. You and Meg have worked wonders with Henry and Bill."

Julia said, "Don't forget about Anna; she has more of a gift than I do. She is amazing with the kids."

Pop leaned back, looked at Julia and said, "Will you listen to us talking about our gifts when the only real gift we have is Meg. She has a gift, we don't. All we can ever hope to be is give her support and nurture Meg's gift and natural talent."

Julia said, "You are absolutely right; this must be about Meg and her friends. I'm embarrassed that we are discussing Meg's gift and effort; and we aren't letting her have a say in any of this. She is old enough, and smart enough, to voice her opinions. In fact, we should do nothing without her approval."

Pop said, "You're right; I should be helping, not dictating. But first, what do you think about buying a big house?"

Julia said, "I think it's a great idea. When you buy the house, I insist on paying for my room and board."

Pop said, "I told you I don't want your money."

Julia said, "Then, use it for the school's needs."

Pop said, "Maybe; I'll think about it. Now, let's talk to Meg."

Pop, Julia and Anna waited for Meg and when she came, she thought something was wrong and asked, "What's going on?"

Pop said, "We have something important to discuss with you; it's about your study group."

Meg asked, "What about it? You aren't going to stop it are you?"

Pop said, "We are concerned that we have taken over your study group without asking what you want; like, we just agreed to add Gloria to the group without asking you first."

Meg said, "I want Gloria to be in it and I want you guys to be in it. I love my study group."

Julia asked, "Isn't it too much? You spend every afternoon, and weekends, with them. You don't have any time for fun things."

Meg asked, "Fun things? My study group is fun. What else would I be doing? Watching TV?"

Pop said, "Good. From now on, you will be involved in every decision that affects the group. The first one is that we need more room for the group; this house isn't big enough. I've been thinking about moving to a larger house so you can have a large classroom. What do you think about that?"

Meg said, "We could use a little more room."

Julia asked, "So, you're okay with moving?"

Meg said, "Yes, as long as I don't have to change schools."

Pop said, "Meg, honey, I may not be able to find a suitable house in this school district; however, we wouldn't move until after the school year."

Meg said, "I would rather stay here than change schools."

Pop asked, "The school means that much to you?"

Meg said, "Yes, I like my school. Miss Mendosa and my friends are all in this school."

Pop said, "Of course. See, you kept me from making a stupid decision. I'll either find a house in this school district or stay in this house."

Meg felt so blessed with Pop, Julia and Anna and thought, *"Pop sure isn't like Jake. I am so lucky I have these guys."*

Their meeting broke up and Pop said to Julia, "I think you and I should talk to Mrs. DeGraff about how we can better structure our curriculum and ask for her opinion about the whole idea."

"I think that's a great idea. Do we take Meg?"

"No, this is something we should do without Meg. Mrs. DeGraff might not be open if Meg is with us."

Pop and Julia met with Mrs. DeGraff and Pop told her what they were doing; and he asked what she thought of the idea.

Mrs. DeGraff said, "I am aware that you are tutoring special needs students and I think that is admirable. Are you thinking of adding more students?"

Pop said, "Not necessarily, we just want to be sure we are doing things the correct way. These kids need help in all subjects, not just English and math. Right now, the parents are involved and helping a lot. It's a lot of effort so we want to do the right thing. We would like to ask for your help in setting up the best curriculum we can."

Mrs. DeGraff asked, "Are any of you qualified teachers?"

Pop said, "None of us are teachers but Miss Carmen Mendosa helps us a lot. Our strength is Meg's gift for working with special needs kids. Mom also works very well with the kids and can devote all her time to that. Julia has a degree in Psychology and is an expert in human behavior; and works as a CSI in the Vallejo police department. Lastly, the parents' participation is a blessing and we could never do it without them."

Mrs. DeGraff asked, "And, what about you? Are you involved?"

Pop laughed and said, "I provide the classroom and handle the finances."

"You are not directly involved with the kids?"

Pop said, "Not as a tutor."

Julia quickly said, "That's not true. Pop spends a lot of time with the kids. He sees that they have fun as well as just studying; and they love him."

Mrs. DeGraff said, "Mister Petrowski, don't sell yourself short. What you do is equally important. Isn't it correct that it was your idea to require parent participation?"

Pop said, "Yes, I suppose it was."

Mrs. DeGraff said, "That is so important. I wish I could impose the same requirement on all families. As for my helping, I can't be directly involved in any capacity. I can say that I believe that what you are doing is a wonderful thing. What I can do is give you one piece of advice; restrict the tutoring to five afternoons a week. Special need kids need a fun day; I recommend Saturdays. Sundays should be free days where none of the kids and families interact; a break from each other and study is vital. Everyone will burn out if you don't. I'm sorry I can offer more. Remember, you are doing something worthwhile for, not only the kids, but their parents as well. Lastly, please know that Meg is a blessing that is extremely rare; and all of you are special people. Thank you for what you are doing."

On their way home, Pop asked, "What do you think?"

Julia said, "I don't know what I expected but she made a good point about the weekends. I agree with her."

Pop said, "So do I. I believe we should ask each family to host a Saturday fun day; like maybe field days. We could tie them to their studies making it educational as well as fun. What do you think about that?"

"I think it's a good idea."

Pop said, "Another thing she did was make me feel a lot better about what we are doing. From now on, we are going to support Meg in any way we can."

Julia said, "I agree. You know, I have really enjoyed the new friends we have. Our lives have certainly gotten a lot more active after Meg came into our lives."

Pop said, "Yeah, I think she might be a keeper."

Julia said, "You think?"

Pop and Julia looked for houses in the area but those that were large enough for their purpose weren't affordable. As they were about to give up, their real estate agent called and told them about a new listing she had; she thought it might work. The house had four bedrooms, a formal dining room plus a very large recreation room on the second floor.

Pop said, "I think it's perfect but it's a little out of my price range."

Julia said, "Pop, it's not out of range if you use my rent money; I want to do this."

Pop said, "It's very tempting but the mortgage payments go for thirty years."

Julia asked, "So?"

Pop said, "I don't want you to feel obligated for that long. You may, one day, want to move away."

Julia said, "The only way that's going to happen is for you to tell me to leave."

Pop said, "I'm not ever going to do that; so, let's show the house to mom and see how she feels about it."

Anna loved the house and said, "Peter, this is perfect. I think you should get it; I can always get a job and help pay for it. You know that I've wanted to go back to work."

Pop said, "Mom, that won't work; we can't do what we want without you being here all the time. I'll make it work; I'll buy it if we can sell our house before someone else buys this house out from under us."

Pop made a contingency offer and it was accepted.

Anna said, "I can't wait to see how Meg reacts to the house when she sees it."

Pop said, "I don't want her to see it before I get it ready. I'm going to do some painting and make a few changes. In fact, I don't want Meg to even know anything about it except that we are selling our house and, after it is sold, we will buy another house. I want it to be a surprise."

Anna and Julia agreed.

Both houses closed escrow on the same day and Pop immediately started working on the new house. Julia enlisted the help of Carmen to make sure they had everything they would need to make the recreation room into a real modern classroom, plus have everything we should have for schooling. The room had white boards on every wall, a large screen TV for showing videos, desks, a bookcase that completely covered the one wall, and a lot cabinets and bookshelves; and of plenty of supplies. In one corner, there was a long table and chairs for lunches.

While the work was being done, Pop got a call from Mrs. DeGraff, "Mister Petrowski, this is Jennifer DeGraff. I've been thinking about you guys and what you are doing; and I would like to help a little. I have drafted a curriculum for you to consider. It offers a well-rounded curriculum and I have drafted a list of books and teaching material that you could buy. I hope it might help."

Pop said, "Thank you; I'm sure it will."

Pop showed the list to Meg, Julia and Carmen and Carmen said, "This will be a great help."

The movers transferred everything to the new house and Anna kept Meg away until Julia called to say the house was ready.

Pop and Julia bought a new dining room set and new bedroom furniture for Meg.

When they got to the house, Meg said, "This is a mansion. Is it really our house?

Pop said, "Yep; and your school."

They went inside and Meg said, "This is nice. I love the dining room and the fireplace in the living room."

Pop said, "Okay, let's go upstairs."

At the top of the stairs was a door on the right that was closed; and there was paper covering something over the top of the door. Meg asked, "What's this room?"

Pop said, "We'll come back to this room after you see your room."

They first went to the master bedroom. Meg said, "You got new furniture."

Pop said, "Nice, huh? This is mom's room and this is Julia's room. Now, your room."

Pop opened the door and Meg started crying. There was a new four-posted bed with a velvet draped canopy over it. The furniture had been bought as a set. There was a window with drapes that matched the ones over the bed.

When Meg was able to stop crying, she said, "I can't believe how beautiful this is. Thank you so much" and hugged Pop very tight.

Pop said, "Now let's go see the last room; I think you might like that one too."

When they got to the door, Pop reached up and removed the paper. There was a sign over the door that had the words "Megan's Academy" carved into it.

Meg asked, "What's this? I don't understand; Megan's Academy?"

Julia said, "It's your special room. Go inside."

Meg opened the door and was blown away. She said, "This is a real classroom!"

Pop said, "Now you and your friends can study with a little style."

Meg said, "This is wonderful. I would like to be home-schooled here."

Pop and Julia were a little surprised that Meg liked her bedroom a lot better than the classroom. Julia, sensing Pop's disappointment whispered, "School isn't as exciting as a new bedroom. She likes them both."

Pop and Julia invited Carmen, the Wades, the Halls, the Fosters, and even Jennifer

DeGraff and her husband, to their open house.

Jennifer took Julia aside and said, "Julia, this is a wonderful thing you and Pop did. I wish that all parents could be half as good as you two."

A week later, Jennifer gave Meg an Oxford English Dictionary for her library. The Wades, Halls and Fosters donated things that Pop and Julia hadn't thought of.

Anna bought a dozen games for their fun. Pop, Anna and Julia were very pleased about how much better Meg's small study group liked their homework sessions.

Meg began her senior year of high school with two more special need students.

Another thing that happened is that Meg's reading to the students taught her much more than if she only went to school. She not only learned more; her comprehension was much greater. Lastly, Meg made a practice of reading the Oxford dictionary aloud to the students. This significantly increased everyone's vocabulary. Meg believed that reading the dictionary was the single most important thing she did.

It was high school graduation for Meg, Bill Foster and Henry. Thanks to Mrs. DeGraff, Meg's study group had grown to seven.

Meg's eighteenth birthday was coming in August and she was having anxiety feelings about becoming an adult. Nobody ever talked about what she would do after graduation. Meg believed that Pop would give her the money from her dad and send her away to college. As graduation neared, Meg became depressed.

One day, Julia said, "Pop, something is bothering Meg; do you have any idea what?"

Pop said, "Mom told me the same thing; and, yes, I've noticed it too. Why don't you ask her; you're better at that than I am."

Julia agreed and, later, took Meg out to lunch to talk to her away from the others. Julia said, "Meg, honey, Pop and I have noticed that something might be bothering you; is there?"

Meg wasn't sure what she should say but Pop had always told her that telling the truth, straight up, was always the best policy.

After hesitating, Meg said, "I'll soon be an adult and I don't know what I am supposed to do after that."

Julia asked, "What do you mean, what will you do? You are going to nursing school; aren't you?"

Meg said, "Yes, but foster care ends when I turn eighteen."

Julia said, "So?"

Meg said, "So, I assume I will have to go out on my own."

Julia sighed and said, "Is that your problem?"

"Yes; and I am having a lot of trouble deciding where I am going to live."

Julia laughed and said, "Honey, you go to school and don't worry about anything else. This is your home. You never have to leave if you don't want to. However, I am sure that some good-looking guy is going to come along one day a sweep you off your feet; then, you will know exactly what you will do."

Meg, looking surprised, asked, "Does Pop feel the same way?"

Juila said, "Of course he does. He loves you very much; don't you know that?"

Meg said, "I know he does; he is almost like my dad."

Julia couldn't wait to talk to Pop.

Julia told Pop what Meg was dealing with and Pop said, "She should have known that she would never have to leave."

Julia said, "Pop, how the hell was she supposed to know? Did you ever tell her?"

Pop sat there a long while before he said, "I guess I never did. I'll take care of this; today!"

That afternoon, after the kids left, Pop said, "Meg, honey, I want to talk to you."

"Okay, when?"

"Right now."

Pop said, "let's walk outside."

As they started walking, Pop said, "Julia told me about your worries. Honey, I am really sorry I haven't talked to you about that. First, I want to say that I love you very much; and that's not just a saying. When I say that, I mean it with all my heart. As far as I am concerned, you are my daughter; not my foster daughter. Being here as a foster child is simply the only legal way I could get you. After I got you, I tried to adopt you but the court wouldn't approve it because I was, I am, a single male. I also want you to know that mom and Julia feel the same way about you. This is your home; forever! If you ever leave, it will be because you want to leave."

Meg asked, "You wanted to adopt me?"

"Yes. I have always wanted you for my daughter."

Meg said, "Thank you so much; I love you too. As far as I am concerned, you are my real father; and always will be."

Pop said, "I would still like to adopt you. I can do that after you become an adult because you can sign the adoption papers yourself."

Meg was surprised and asked, "You can really adopt another adult?"

Pop smiled and said, "Yes, you can. Megan Fowler, will you become my legal daughter?"

Meg hugged Pop and said, "Yes, I would love that. Would that make Anna my real grandmother?"

"Yes, if that's what you want."

Meg asked, "Can I change my name to Petrowski?"

"Of course, you can. I would love that."

Meg looked into Pop's eyes and said, I love you, dad."

That did it! Tears ran down Pop's cheeks and he said, "I love you, too; Megan Petrowski."

Pop and Meg went back to the house and Meg found Anna; she said, "Hi, grandma. I love you" and gave Anna a big hug.

Anna asked, "What's all this about? Grandma?"

Meg said, "Dad, that's Pop, is going to adopt me when I turn eighteen; that will make you my real grandma."

Anna began crying and said, "It sure does, honey."

Ten days after Meg's birthday, her new birth certificate came. Meg ran to Anna and said, "It's official; I am a Petrowski, grandma."

Pop threw a party to celebrate the adoption. Pop announced that Meg was now his legal daughter; named Megan Ann Petrowski. Pop said, "Another announcement is that my daughter will be going to nursing school in two weeks. Let's all wish her well."

After the cheering stopped, Pop said, "Miss Petrowski, come with your father."

Pop took her to one of the garage doors, gave Meg a garage door opener and said, "Push the button."

Meg pushed the button, the door raised and there was a red 1984 Toyota Celica Supra. Pop said, "You will need your own wheels when you start school."

Meg squealing, hugged Pop and said, "I sure love my dad."

Just before school started, Jennifer DeGraff asked if she could send six new special needs kids to Meg's study group since the others were graduating.

Meg asked Pop about it and he said, "Meg, it's important that you devote yourself to your own studies. Nursing is a very demanding course; the last thing you want to do is take away from your studies."

"I think I can do it. I did it throughout high school and it didn't hurt my grades; and I also made up a whole grade."

Pop said, "If Julia will continue helping you, and you charge something for doing it, I say okay."

Meg said, "Thank you; how much should I charge?"

Pop said, "How about 5 dollars a day; and limit the time to one and one-half hours, five days per week?"

Meg asked, "Why not weekends?"

Pop said, "Meg, you need to do your homework on weekends."

Meg called Jennifer, told her the terms and Jennifer said, "That sounds very reasonable; I'll discuss it with the parents and get back to you."

After the families were told that Meg started charging for her time, two students didn't join. That left Meg with four paying students. Meg thought that, in fairness, that all students would have to pay. Since it was merely a token charge, all last year's students agreed to pay.

Meg tried to get Julia to take half of the money but Julia refused. Julia said, "Use the money for school needs."

During the first year of nursing school, Meg refused to take additional students; there were numerous requests because Meg began building a reputation as a good special needs tutor.

One day, Jennifer asked to talk to Meg, Pop and Julia.

Jennifer said, "I've been giving Meg a lot of thought and came to the conclusion that Meg should consider becoming a teacher instead of a nurse. She is a gifted teacher, especially with special needs children. That's why I wanted to talk to all of you. Is that something you would consider?"

Pop looked at Meg but said nothing. Meg finally said, "I have always had my heart set on becoming a nurse. I like tutoring part-time. After I become a nurse, I can still continue part-time tutoring. Besides, I need a master's degree to teach, don't I?"

Jennifer said, "You can teach young children with a bachelor's degree but having a master's will let you teach anywhere."

Meg said, "Thank you Mrs. DeGraff but I want to stay in nursing school."

Pop said, "The lady has spoken. We appreciate your believing in Meg and thank you for thinking about her best interest. I must honor her wishes."

Jennifer said, "I understand; thank you for hearing me out."

Meg graduated nursing school and, after the graduation ceremony, Meg said, "Pop, Julia, grandma, I have an announcement. I applied to Berkely and have been accepted into their teaching program. I've decided that I want to teach full-time. Is this okay with you guys?"

Pop quickly said, "I think that's great. What about your tutoring?"

Meg said, "I definitely want to continue with it. I am going to specialize in teaching special need kids; and my nursing schooling helped me understand a lot more than I ever would have otherwise. I am glad that I finished nursing school."

Julia said, "Meg, I am so proud of you."

Without thinking, Meg said, "Thank you, mom."

As soon as Meg said those words, she stunned herself and said, "I'm sorry, Julia, I don't know why I called you mom."

Julia's heart was pounding and she said, "Honey, that didn't bother me; it made me feel honored."

Julia went to Meg and hugged her. While they were embracing, Anna said, "That looks wonderful."

Pop said, "That's a mother and daughter if I ever saw any."

From that moment on, Julia and Meg's relationship went to a much deeper level. For all intents and purposes, they became

mother and daughter; it didn't go un-
noticed by Pop either.

15

Pop and Julia were working on a crime scene and, as they worked, Pop's mind couldn't focus on the crime scene, he was thinking about his life; how almost perfect it was and what was missing from it. Everything seemed perfect; he was Meg's dad, Julia was like Meg's daughter, mom was like her grandma and we all love each other; and we live in the same house.

However, Pop realized what was wrong and that the only thing wrong was him; further, only he could make this picture perfect.

They finished working the crime scene and Pop said, "Hey, Julia, how about you and I spend the weekend in Reno; just you and me?"

Julia said, "Sounds great to me; what's the occasion?"

"No special occasion, you know what they say; all work and no play."

Pop and Julia left at noon on Friday, checked into the hotel and went to dinner.

At dinner, Pop asked, "Have I told you lately that I love you?"

Julia said, "Not since yesterday."

"I love you very much and I have something to say. I am guilty of being the biggest fool on the whole damned planet.

I always wanted to have a perfect family and a perfect life and the only reason I don't have it now is my own stupidity. My perfect life is all around me but I didn't realize it until now."

Julia said, "Your life looks pretty perfect to me; what in the world more could you want?"

Pop said, "I want you."

Julia said, "It seems to me that you already have me."

"Julia, I love you very much and I want you in my life as long as I live. Will you marry me?"

Julia never expected this. Pop had always avoided anything that might lead to marriage. He always said that he was a confirmed bachelor.

Julia hadn't answered Pop yet and he began to squirm in his seat. Seeing this, Julia said, "I guess I had better answer you, huh?"

Pop said, "It would sure help a lot if you did; you are killing me. My entire life is passing over my eyes."

Julia said, "I would love to marry you."

Pop stood, looked around at the people in the restaurant and shouted, "She said yes! She said yes!"

The weekend was like a honeymoon and Pop said, "I wish I had done this a long time ago. I've been so damned foolish. I don't understand why you stayed with me all this time."

Julia said, "Because I have loved you from the time we met and this was the only way I could have you; so, I stayed."

Pop lowered his head and said, "Please forgive me; and, for the record, I have loved you from the time we met."

Julia said, "All's well that ends well."

Back at home, as everyone sat in the living room, Pop said, "I have an announcement; Julia is getting married."

Everyone was shocked and Meg asked, "Who are you marrying?"

Julia smiled and said, "Your father."

Meg jumped up and asked, "Are you and dad really getting married?"

Pop said, "Yes, if I don't screw up."

Meg, looking at Julia, asked, "Does that mean I can call you mom?"

Julia said, "Honey, you can if that's what you want."

Meg said, "I really do, mom."

As soon as the excitement calmed, Anna said, "I also have an announcement to make. Since Meg is an adult, I am going back to work."

Julia asked, "You really want to go to work?"

Anna said, "I've always wanted to work but Peter wouldn't hear of it. Now, I am exercising my authority. I have a job offer to work in my doctor's office as her receptionist and administrator."

Pop said, "Let's talk about that later; now, we need to plan the wedding. I want Julia to have the wedding of her dreams. Will you all help plan it?"

Meg shouted, "Yes; I want to help. Can I be in it?"

Julia said, "You are my maid of honor; and I want a formal wedding."

Pop said, "The only people that will be attending the wedding who aren't cops will be Jennifer DeGraff and her family, Carmen Mendosa and her fiancé, The Wades, Halls and Fosters."

Anna said, "That should make it easy to plan."

Pop said, "There's one more thing; since we are all adults here, Julia is moving into my room now; if that's okay."

Anna said, "It's about time."

And, they were married.

Meg's Academy continued through college and added more students. That was all Meg wanted to handle especially now that Anna had a job.

Meg was graduating from Berkely with her bachelor's degree. She has also registered for the Master's program in special education.

Meg's study group now included nine students; she could have twenty if she could handle them but decided against it.

Meg had given this a lot of thought and had finally concluded that she wanted to open her own school for special needs students after she graduated.

Meg said, "Dad, I want to make my school my career. Do you think that me opening an accredited special needs school is feasible?"

Pop said, "I never thought about that. A full-time-accredited school is more than a school; it's also a business. I'll give it some thought."

Pop looked into the requirements for accreditation of the school and learned that they would need to have a seasoned teacher head the school. Meg couldn't even be listed as a teacher until after she had her Master's degree. Julia was an accredited psychologist; but she would have to work at the school full-time. Further, the school would require additional teachers and staff. First, and foremost, the school would need paying students; not the token amount Meg now charged her students.

Pop knew that he had a lot of work to do. He talked to Julia about working for the school instead of the police department. Julia said, "I love working with the kids but I like my job."

Pop said, "I am having a hard time with this. I want to support Meg but I don't think I would let her do it without you. Meg leans on you more than you know."

Julia said, "Now, you put me on the spot."

Pop said, "Don't feel that way. You should only join the school if you really want to do it as a profession. Meg can simply teach in an existing school."

Julia gave the idea some thought and said, "Pop, I think we should explore the feasibility of the school. If it looks feasible, I will do it."

Pop asked, "Are you sure you really want to do it or is it for Meg's benefit?"

Julia said, "I thought about it and I believe that leaving police work to teach would eliminate all the dark shit we have to deal with every day. Teaching those kids will be a joy."

Pop said, "Okay, I'll try to figure out how to make it feasible."

After a lot of research and discussions, Pop told Meg, "I think I know how to make your school a reality; if you still want to do it?"

Meg said, "Yes and I want Carmen to be the head of the school; if she will do it."

Pop said, "She would certainly qualify so let's ask her what she thinks."

They first told Carmen what their plan was to get her opinion.

Carmen said, "It sounds great but Meg can't get certification from the school board. She is great with the kids but she doesn't have professional experience; even though she has good skills."

Pop said, "Actually, Carmen, we already learned that; now, the big question, will you consider joining us as head of the school?"

Carmen said, "I am honored but I don't have professional experience with special needs teaching."

Pop said, "I disagree. You are a qualified teacher and you have worked with Meg for the past four years teaching special need students. As far as I am concerned, that was professional experience; you just didn't charge for your services. I can get Jennifer DeGraff to write a letter to that effect."

Carmen said, "This has taken me by complete surprise; but I will think about

307

it. If I decide against it, I believe I could recommend a couple of teachers that would qualify."

Meg said, "But, I want you, Miss Mendosa."
Later, Meg asked, "Dad, do you think Miss Mondoza will do it?"

Pop said, "I don't know. This is a very big professional decision for her. Starting a new school is very risky; and she will, most likely, have to take a pay cut. I believe we have to be prepared for her to say no; I'm sorry."

Meg said, "I don't want to do it without her. If she says no, I'll just get my master's and teach."

Pop asked, "Are you sure?"

Meg said, "I'm sure. I know my school will work with her but I won't risk it with anyone else."

Two days later, Carmen said, "I'm very sorry, Meg; but I can't do this. Otherwise, I will help you in any way I can."

Meg said, "I understand. It's okay. Maybe one day." Carmen said, "Maybe one day."
A year later, the school year ended for the summer and Meg had twelve students signed up for the summer. Carmen agreed to work with Meg for the summer.

During the school year, Meg met Nolan Skyler. Nolan was in several of Meg's classes and was getting his doctorate in special education. There was an immediate mutual attraction but Meg's past came barging back to the surface. She believed that her having been raped by her stepdad killed her desire to have sex.

Nolan persisted until Meg agreed to date him. They became close friends but their relationship remained platonic.

One day, Meg and Nolan were standing under a tree on the campus and Nolan kissed Meg.

Meg felt strange sensations and her knees weakened.

"Why did you do that?"
 "Meg, I am crazy about you. I don't want to be merely friends."

Meg said, "It's friends or nothing. I'm not into sex."

"Meg, I didn't mean that; but I do want to kiss you, hold you and hold hands. I want you to be my girlfriend."

Meg said, "I don't know how to be a girlfriend and I've never had a boyfriend. You are the first one that ever kissed me."

Meg, immediately knew that he would think she never had sex; and it bothered her to let him think that. She needed to talk to Julia.

After she got home, Meg got Julia aside and said, "Mom, I need to talk to you; in private."

They went to Meg's room and Meg said, "I just got kissed for the first time and I got a lot of weird feelings. I had trouble breathing and my knees were weak. What does that mean?"

Julia was very relieved to hear this. She and Pop had discussed Meg's lack of interest in boys, or men. Pop said, "Maybe she is a lesbian."

Julia said, "I don't believe that. I believe it's all about the sexual abuse by Jake. It ruined her self-esteem and turned her against intimacy. I think she simply found someone who rings her bell; she is normal after all.

Julia said, "It's your hormones raging; and it's about time."

Meg asked, "What do you mean?"

"I mean that Jake didn't ruin you. It means that there is nothing wrong with your sex drive. Who is this knight in shining armor?"

"He is a friend from school; his name is Nolan Skyler. He is getting his doctorate in special needs teaching this year. He wants me to be his girlfriend; and he says he is not just after sex. I don't know whether to believe him or not."

Julia asked, "How long have you been friends?"

"This whole school year."

Julia asked, "And, he hasn't tried to have sex with you?"

"No, he only kissed me yesterday; for the first time."

Julia said, "He sounds like a perfect gentleman to me. Would you like to be his girlfriend?"

Meg said, "I do but what if he does want sex, what should I do?"

Julia said, "Meg, you are twenty-one years old. Just follow your heart; it knows what to do and when to do it. Just remember that you have to keep from getting pregnant. Maybe you should go on the pill; that way, when the time comes, you will be prepared."

"Mom, that doesn't help me know how to handle it."

Julia said, "Meg, just enjoy being with him and let nature take its course. Trust me, you will know what to do; and when to do it. In the meantime, be happy and have fun. By the way, bring this gentleman home so we can meet him."

Meg said, "I believe that I have to tell Nolan about what Jake did to me; but I'm afraid he will not have anything to do with me after that. I was also thinking that, maybe, I should never tell him. There is no way he could ever learn about it. What should I do?"

Julia asked, "Meg, what would Pop say to you?"

After a pause to think about it, Meg said, "Dad would say, "Always tell the truth"; but if I don't tell him, I won't be telling a lie."

"Meg, you know very well that, to not tell him, is also a lie."

Meg said, "Yes, I know. I'll tell him tomorrow."

Julia said, "Good girl. If you two are meant to be together, it won't matter to Nolan. If it does matter to him, he's not the one for you."

Meg tossed and turned all night long thinking about how to tell Nolan and wondering what he would say and how he would feel.

The next day Meg called Nolan and asked, "Nolan, can we get together tonight? I need to talk to you."

"Sure; where?"

Meg said, "At the campus on our bench; at eight."

Meg saw Nolan sitting on the bench as she walked toward it.

"Hi."

Nolan said, "Hi. What's up; and why here?"

Meg said, "I need to tell you why I can't be your girlfriend. I have a past that isn't very nice and you deserve someone better than me."

Nolan looked at Meg and asked, "What?"

Meg told Nolan the whole truth about her mom, Jake and his physical and sexual abuse. When she finished, she sighed and said, "Now, I've told you; and I understand if you don't want anything more to do with me. I believe I owed you the truth about me."

Nolan asked, "I'm the first guy that ever kissed you?"

Meg said, "Yes. I tried to keep you from doing it but you sneaked the kiss."

Nolan's first reaction was to feel sorry for Meg but he quickly admired her for who she was; and that made him love her more.

Nolan said, "Meg, I am honored that I am the first one you let kiss you. As far as I am concerned, that makes you a virgin. Meg, I want to be your boyfriend."

Meg asked, "You still want me?"

Nolan leaned over, kissed Meg and said, "You have my heart and soul; I am helpless."
Meg was feeling wonderful and thought, *"This is my guy. I can't believe he loves me and I love him, too."*

Meg then kissed Nolan and said, "You have to come meet my family; right now!"

Nolan said, "I would love that; let's go."

They got home and Meg said, "Nolan, this is my dad, everyone calls him Pop, and my mom, Julia and my grandmother, Anna."

Nolan was confused and Pop noticed it.

Pop said, "I think Meg hasn't told you everything. We aren't her biological parents, I adopted her. Actually, Julia and I arrested her when she was 14. Then, she stole our hearts."

Pop continued telling Nolan the complete story up to today.

After Pop finished with Meg's story, Nolan told them his life story.

He was from an upper-class family and was going to teach in a special need school.

After Nolan finished his story, he said that Meg was a special, and gifted, person; and he loved what she has done for those kinds of kids. Finally, he said, "Folks, it was very nice meeting you. It's time I went home."

After Nolan left, Pop said, "I like him."

Julia said, "I do too."

Meg said, "I'm glad."

Anna said, "Count me into his fan club. I think he's a keeper."

Meg was so happy she could hardly contain herself. She had never felt this way before.

The next day, Nolan said, "Okay, Meg, you now have to meet my folks. I want you to come Friday night for dinner."

Meg said, "I guess turnabout is fair play. I'll go."

At home, Meg asked Julia, "What should I wear? I want to make a good first impression."

Julia said, "Just make sure your clothes are clean."

Meg said, "I'm serious."

Julia said, "So am I. Meg, the last thing you want to do is go there looking like someone you are not; be yourself. Wear your regular clothes."

When Meg came into the room to meet Nolan's parents, she wore her newest jeans, a blouse and Sketchers shoes. The jeans were full-fit and loose. The blouse had short sleeves, was multi-colored and buttoned all the way except for the last button. She wore tiny heart earrings and her hair was pulled back; and she wore only a little makeup; just enough to highlight her features. She looked like she walked off the cover of a 1950s teen magazine; a wholesome young woman.

Nolan's mom, Vivian, was surprised. She didn't know what she expected Meg to look like except she never expected her to look like this. Meg reminded her of Betty Anderson on the 50s TV show, Father Knows Best.

Nolan's dad, had in his mind that Nolan would bring some sexy little chick home and was very pleased with what he saw.

The evening went very well and Meg liked the Skyler's.

On the way home, Meg said, "I like your parents."

Nolan said, "They liked you as well; I can tell."

Meg said, "You have to tell them all about me. They have to know everything."

Nolan asked, "Why?"

Meg said, "Because they have to accept me for who and what I am; they must know everything. I can't have any secrets; I can't even keep dating you if you don't tell them everything. If you don't feel like doing it, I will."

Nolan said, "Okay but I know they will think the same way I do."

Meg said, "Good; then, it won't hurt, will it?"

Nolan said, "I should tell them when you aren't there."

Nolan told his parents and they both remained silent. After a while, Nolan simply left without anyone saying anything. After Nolan left, Paul asked, "What do you think about her now?"

Vivian said, "My heart goes out to her. She has endured so much abuse; it's a wonder she survived it. I believe she is to be admired. Remember, Nolan said that she insisted that we know all about her past. That tells me a lot about her character. I like her."

Paul said, "No wonder she is devoted to helping special need kids. She is a saint in the making, if you asked me."

Vivian said, "I'm glad that Nolan chose her."

Paul laughed and said, "Honey, Nolan hasn't married her; he's just dating her."

Vivian said, "Paul, Nolan loves her; can't you see that?"

"Maybe."

16

After receiving his doctorate, Nolan was going to take a job teaching at a special needs school in Berkeley.

Meg received her Master's degree and now had to decide what she would do next.

Meg told Nolan about her wish to start her own school and he said, "That's a fantastic idea; I think you should do it if you can."

Meg said, "If I did, would you work for me?"

Nolan asked, "Where would you get enough students to start a school?"

"Getting students will be no problem, if we could get my 9th grade teacher to head up the school."

Nolan said, "Ask her."

Meg said, "I did a year ago and she turned me down. She said it was too risky for her."

Nolan said, "Ask again; she might change her mind. If I join you; and if Julia also came on board, she might see that the risk is a lot less."

Meg said, "Even if Carmen agreed, we would have to pay her a lot more money than I could pay you."

Nolan said, "I have no problem with that. Ask her again."

Meg said, "I'll talk to dad first. If he says okay, I'll ask her again."

Meg told Pop and Julia that she wanted to start her own school; if she could. She said, "With my five years of experience tutoring the kids, a Master's degree, plus Nolan and his Doctorate, we might get certified for a k through 8ᵗʰ grade school. What do you guys think?"

Julia looked at Pop and said, "You can count me in with my added qualifications.

I'm a psychologist and have experience teaching special need kids. That's a lot of qualifications. The problem is going to be where do we teach? How do we show that we can be a viable school?"

Meg said, "I can ask Nolan's dad; he is a CEO of some big company."

Pop said, "Good idea; and don't forget that you have a little working capital."

Meg disgustingly said, "That dirty money?"

Julia said, "Yes, that's dirty money but can you think of a better use for it than helping your kids? Think about all the good that dirty money can do."

Meg said, "I never looked at it like that. I like that idea."

Meg told Nolan what Pop and Julia had said, and he said, "I'll talk to dad."

Later, Nolan said, "Dad told me that we should have a basic business plan and a place picked out to locate the school. If the plan indicates that the school is financially viable, you might have a chance; and, if you can recruit Miss Mendosa, I'd say it would be a done deal."

Meg and Nolan drafted their plan, which included an old store in a strip mall to be the school. Nolan gave the plan to his dad and his dad helped him rewrite it. They now had a professional looking business plan. Armed with their plan, Meg called Carmen and asked if she and Nolan could meet with her.

Meg and Nolan met with Carmen; and she said, "Funny, I was about to call you.

What did you ever do about starting your own school?"

Meg said, "I put it off until I got my Master's. I have it now, and I have a partner. This is Nolan Skyler. He has his doctorate in teaching special need kids."

Nolan said, "Hi, Miss Mendosa; pleased to meet you. Meg talks about you all the time."

"I hope most of it was good."

Meg asked, "What were you going to call about?"

Carmen said, "I wanted to ask if you decided what you want to do about your school."

Meg said, "That's funny; I wanted to talk to you about the same thing. Nolan and I have decided that we want to start a school; and that we are almost ready. We have a business plan that I would like to show you; and, hopefully, you will critique it for us. You will also notice that the plan was written showing you as the school master; I had to show a school master. Will you at least read it and give us your critique?"

Carmen said, "Of course I will but, before I do, I want to say that I am happy that you want to go ahead with the school and I am flattered that you still want me. I want to say, before I read the plan, that I changed my mind and I am definitely interested in joining you. This area badly needs a school like yours."

Meg said, "That's wonderful. We came hoping our plan would convince you to join us. As you can see, the name of the school is Megan's Academy. Dad named the school when he put that plaque over my classroom."

It took Carmen an hour to read the highlights of the plan. After she finished, she looked up at Meg and said, "Meg, this looks great. Julia is actually willing to quit her job and join you?"

Meg said, "Yes, and she is very excited about it. What do you think our chances of getting certification are?"

Carmen said, "I've given that a lot of thought and I think the odds are even. However, in the case of special need children, especially grades k through 8th, certification may not be necessary. I believe there would be enough students that won't be going on to high school to require certification; but the best of all worlds would be that you are accredited."

With Carmen on the staff, Meg applied to the school board for certification.

Today was when they would learn the school board's decision.

Meg, Pop, Julia, Nolan and Carmen went to the hearing.

Meg bought a new outfit for the occasion. She wanted to look professional so she bought an expensive business outfit.

After she was dressed, Meg said, "I look like a school principal."

Pop said, "That's the way you are supposed to look. You look beautiful."

Carmen said, "Meg, it is important that you don't worry about their decision; we are going to have our school either way. Show them that you are a self-confident professional young woman that is opening a new school, one way or the other; certification is simply the frosting on the cake."

Carmen's words made a big difference; Meg's confidence soared. Meg led the way into the hearing room with her head held high, shoulders back and she was truly confident.

Meg looked stunning in a conservative way and had a commanding attitude, yet graceful.

After they sat down, the chairwoman called the meeting to order and said, "Miss Petrowski, we have reviewed your request for certification and your business plan. I must tell you the board has reservations about certifying a startup school."

Meg's heart began beating faster and her confidence began to waiver.

The chairwoman continued, "Your, and Mister Skyler's educational qualifications are extraordinary but you both are very young. However, your business plan looks very good and your partners, Miss Archer and Miss Mendosa are more than qualified; and bring a lot of valuable experience to your school. I am pleased to tell you that the school board has approved your school for certification. This meeting is now adjourned.

Congratulations; now prove worthy of our trust in you."

17

It was opening day for Megan's Academy. The school had two large classrooms; one for k through 5th and one for 6th through 8th.

There were twenty-three students. 14 students in the k to 5th group and 9 in 6th to 8th group.

Pop and Anna were there for the opening and Anna said, "This is a wonderful thing."

Pop said, "It makes me very glad I arrested that kid and made her my daughter."

Over the next four years, Megan's Academy flourished and now it was graduation day for Meg. Today, she was receiving her doctorate in special education.

There was a celebration planned for after the ceremony for later that night; it was going to be a formal ball.

Meg, Julia and Anna went to a spa, had their hair and makeup done by a professional.

Julia said, "Meg, I want you to get dressed first."

Meg got dressed and Julia said, "You look fabulous."

Meg said, "That doesn't look like me."

Anna said, "Oh yes it does. Meg, you are a very beautiful young lady. It's time the butterfly came out of the cocoon."

Meg said, "I feel like Cinderella; and that tonight, I'll turn back into an ugly duckling."

Julia said, "Meg, you are going to knock their eyes out tonight; not to mention what it's going to do to Nolan."

That night, after they all were dressed and ready, Pop said, "You and I aren't going yet."

Meg asked, "Why not?"

Pop said, "You are the one being honored; you are supposed to come in after everyone else has been seated; and waiting an appropriate amount of time. I will then walk you into the ballroom on my arm. That's the way these things are properly done. I want to show off my beautiful and amazing daughter."

Meg said, "You are very biased but I love you anyway."

As Meg and Pop came into the room, the band stopped playing and Julia was at the microphone. She said, "Ladies and Gentlemen, I present my daughter Megan Petrowski and her father Peter."

Nolan couldn't believe his eyes. Meg wore a form-fitting dark blue gown that was off one shoulder. The gown showed just the right amount of cleavage; and Meg was well endowed. She wore small single pearl earrings and a pearl necklace. Meg was simply remarkably beautiful. Best of all, Meg felt beautiful for the first time in her life.

Meg and Pop sat down and Nolan said, "You are the most beautiful woman I've ever seen."

Meg said, "Thank you, dear."

Everyone at the table remarked about how good Meg looked. The band began playing a slow song and Nolan asked,

"May I have the honor of the first dance, my lady?"

Meg whispered, "I don't know how to dance."
Nolan whispered back, "Just walk slowly to be music and I will direct you. It's a piece of cake. Come."

Meg reluctantly followed Nolan to the dance floor and he began guiding her. "Just move your feet very slightly in the direction I push or pull you. It's very easy. All you have to do is relax and follow my lead."

Sure enough, Meg started flowing with the music. She was thrilled to be moving in Nolan's strong hands. The only trouble was that Meg's knees were shaking as her feelings flowed throughout her body. She knew that she was very much sexually aroused.

After the dance, Pop asked, "May your father have this dance?"

Meg said, "Dad, may we wait for the next slow song?"

"Sure thing."
Meg didn't want to say that she was so aroused that she couldn't dance.

The next slow song began and Pop led Meg onto the dance floor. As they danced, Meg said, "I love you so much. Thank you for everything you've done for me. I am so proud that I can call you my dad, even though you aren't."

Pop said, "Megan Petrowski, I am your dad. Dads aren't made by sperm; they are made by love. Nobody can love you more than I do."

Meg, in her heart, knew that what Pop said was true. After the dance, Meg said, "I love you, dad."

When it became time to close the ball, Meg thanked everyone for their support over the past four years and for her family for saving her life and adopting her.

Meg said, "It's been a very long journey and I have been lucky beyond belief."

That night, as Meg lay in bed, she thought about Nolan. They have known each other for six years and Meg concluded that it was time for her to have sex with him. Every time he kissed her, the desire increased. She believed that Nolan wanted to go to another level in their relationship but hasn't tried yet. Meg thought, *"I wish Nolan could be here now, in my bed, making love to me; but I'm the reason Nolan isn't and he hasn't even tried to have sex with me; I told him to never try. I guess it's up to me to take the initiative."*

Meg didn't want the first time she had sex with Nolan to be a one-night thing. She wanted a weekend.

The next day, Meg said to Nolan, "I would like to ask you for a date for this Friday night."

Nolan said, "I would be most happy to go out with you." Wondering what this was all about, he thought, "*She's got something up her sleeve; but who cares.*"

Meg's plan was to surprise Nolan by taking him to a hotel and spending the entire weekend there. She went to the extent of buying Nolan underwear and two sets of clothes. She planned to only tell him where to drive and have him turn into the hotel.

At dinner, Nolan said, "I need to go to the men's room."

After returning to the table, the waiter brought a bottle of champagne. Meg asked, "What's the champagne for?"

Nolan pulled a box out of his pocket and said, "Will you please marry me? If you don't I think I will die."

Meg was stunned but her heart melted. She said, "Okay."

Nolan said, "Praise God; thank you."

Meg thought, *"That makes tonight all the more special."*

Nolan reached over and kissed meg. Next, he put the ring on her finger.

Meg looked at the ring and said, "It's beautiful."

Nolan said, "I've wanted to do this for a long time but you had so much on your plate; I waited as long as I could."

Meg said, "The timing is perfect. I love you for waiting for me to get my head straight."

After dinner, Nolan pulled the car onto the street to go home and Meg said, "Make a U-turn and go in the other direction."

"Where are we going?"

Meg said, "Remember, I asked for this date before you upstaged me."

Nolan said, "I would say that I am sorry but I would be lying. Where to?"

"Just drive; I'll tell you where to turn."
Meg said, "Turn right at the next driveway."

Nolan turned right into the front of a major hotel.

Meg said, "Pull up to the front door and park."

Nolan asked, "Are we going to have a drink?"

Meg said, "Get the suitcase out of the trunk. The reservation is in your name."

Nolan was now getting his hopes high. *"Is this what I think it is?"*

Nolan sat the suitcase down and said,
"Reservation for Nolan Skyler."

Nolan signed in and they went to their
room; all the while not speaking.

After Nolan closed the door, Meg said, "I
thought it was about time we took our
relationship to a higher level. Unless you
object, we are staying here until Monday
morning. You have clothes in the
suitcase."

Nolan said, "I have no objections."

Both of their hormones were raging and
they made love for the first time.

The weekend was spent talking about
their future mixed in with bouts of sex.

Sunday night, Meg asked, "When do you
think we should have a baby?"

Nolan said, as a question, "Right away?"

Meg said, "I think right away is the perfect time."

Everyone was pleased about their getting married and looked forward to planning the wedding.

Epilog

Meg got pregnant and had a boy fifteen months after they were married. They named him Peter Paul Skyler; after Pop and Nolan's dad.

One year later, Grace Julia was born.

Two years after that, Carmen hired a teacher that had Tourette Syndrome; she married him a year later.

Three years later, Anna married the father of one of the school's Down Syndrome students.

Ten years later, Megan's Academy had grown to 420 students and a demand that was growing.

They broke ground on their next school which would expand to include high school.

Meg and her academy had become a legend within the special needs community. Her academy set new standards for special needs curriculum and developed many new physical and mental therapies to improve the lives of the afflicted.

Twenty years later, Pop retired from the Vallejo PD.

Made in the USA
Columbia, SC
02 March 2023

13096010R00189